PARTY AND REPRESENTATION

Published simultaneously in Great Britain
by Prentice-Hall International, London

PARTY AND REPRESENTATION

Legislative Politics in Pennsylvania

Frank J. Sorauf

ATHERTON PRESS
A Division of Prentice-Hall, Inc.
70 Fifth Avenue, New York 11

1963

PARTY AND REPRESENTATION
Legislative Politics in Pennsylvania

Frank J. Sorauf

Copyright © 1963 by Prentice-Hall, Inc.
Atherton Press, New York, New York

Published simultaneously in Great Britain by
Prentice-Hall International, Inc.
28 Welbeck Street, London W.1, England

Atherton Press, A Division of Prentice-Hall, Inc.
70 Fifth Avenue, New York 11, New York

Library of Congress Catalog Card Number: 63-13840
Printed in the United States of America 65175

212573

The American Political Science Association Series

OTHER SERIES PUBLICATIONS

Nation-Building
KARL W. DEUTSCH AND WILLIAM J. FOLTZ,
EDITORS

The Future of Political Science
HAROLD D. LASSWELL

Preface

Since Chapter 1 and the appendixes contain statements of the goals and procedures of this study, it is not necessary to repeat them at length here. This book embodies my convictions of the necessity to study political parties as political organizations with organizational characteristics, functions, and activities. To that end, I have studied the operating political party as it enters the process of representation at crucial points.

By the very nature of the project I have had to develop new types of data with which to study the parties. Large sections of the study rest on data other than the usual vote totals, census data, and legislative roll calls. Many of those data came from field interviews in the state capital and many of the Pennsylvania counties. For many of the data, I have had to develop new categories and typologies. For these reasons, especially, I have tried to set down my procedures carefully. They may suggest criticisms, improvements, and points of departure for other scholars. I know that I would like to have known at the beginning of this study what I had learned by its conclusion.

My debts in this study are numerous and great. I am, first of all, grateful to the Committees on State Politics and Political Behavior of the Social Science Research Council for the grants which supported this work. For their excellent interviewing, I am indebted to Mrs. Kenneth Masters, Thomas R. Dye, and Fred R. Wentzel. They also contributed many valuable suggestions and insights in the course of their work. I am similarly obliged to James Skok, Bradlee Karan, Norman Cohen, and Robert Abraham for their thoughtful and conscientious assistance in what were certainly the most tedious aspects of the project. The reference librarians of the Pattee Library of the Pennsylvania State University, and especially Mrs. Harold Fishbein, were immensely helpful. My typists, Mrs. Roy Morey, Carol Halvorson Blowers, and Mrs. William Lemons, saw the manuscript carefully through several drafts. The staffs of the numerical analysis and data processing services of Pennsylvania State University and the University of Arizona educated me most capably in the mysteries of their arts. I also thank my friend and former colleague, Neal Riemer, for his suggestions and encouragement when I most needed them. Finally, to the anonymous hundreds of Pennsylvania politicians and political observers who so patiently gave us of their time and wisdom, my special thanks.

Frank J. Sorauf

Minneapolis, Minnesota
July 1963

Contents

Contents

List of Tables

PARTY AND REPRESENTATION

1 • Introduction

The American political party has a remarkable power to baffle not only foreign observers, but knowledgeable Americans as well. It does not usually enroll its loyalists into party membership, and party registration totals often provide only the most casual clue to the actual support a party can expect in elections. It rarely maintains any sort of continuous political activity; after a spasm of activity at election time, it lapses into a recuperative dormancy until the next one. Its affairs usually rest in the hands of a small cadre of party officials who remain independent of the nominal national leadership. And so informal is its approach to political principles that it rarely undertakes a systematic statement of its commitments.

How, then, does one describe a party whose membership he cannot identify, whose activity for long periods is a studied inactivity, whose fragmented direction remains in the hands of hundreds of local oligarchs, and whose failure to enunciate a distinguishing ideology is endemic? Primarily by not looking for more than meets the eye. Much more than other democratic parties, those of the United States are essentially electing organizations. It is almost exclusively through the contesting of elections that they perform their functions of organizing political power and clarifying political choice.

It is easily granted that the major American parties function chiefly as electing organizations, that they are pre-eminently coalitions for the capture of public office. Yet, the operation of the American party in its classic function has not been thoroughly studied. Any number of scholarly works have dealt with the party as a coalition of the socioeconomic, regional, racial, and ethnic groups making up its electorate. Others have dealt with the parties as images in the consciousness of voters and groups of voters and as objects of their professed loyalties. Still others, especially the studies of the flamboyant urban machines and bosses, have described the party as a militant organization. But the instances in which these works have looked directly at the parties in their attempts to control and influence the election of candidates—at the parties in their electing function—have been rare indeed.

In fact, "party" as an organized recruiter and elector of candidates has been conspicuously missing in many of the recent excellent studies of American voting and electoral politics. The sophisticated sample survey—a successful tool for uncovering voter preferences and attitudes—must of necessity by-pass the party organization in action. Furthermore, the centralized politics of a presidential election offer a generally unsatisfactory occasion for observing the functions of a decentralized party system.

Primarily, then, this book studies the political parties as they go about the business of electing candidates to office. It will focus on those points at which the party intervenes in the long process by which we choose and supervise our legislators. How does the party find a candidate? Does it actively recruit him or merely suffer and ratify the hopes of the self-appointed? What attempts does it make to dominate the direct primary and keep for itself control over access to the general election contest? To ask these questions of a party is to assess its power to state the alternatives

2

that confront the voter in an election. At the same time it is, at least implicitly, to relate the parties' attempts to exclude powerful nonparty elites in the community from a share of the control over the nomination and election processes.

The role of the parties in the recruitment and election of candidates to office bisects the entire representational system of a democracy. In its selecting function, the party straddles the gulf between constituency and candidate, attending to constituency demands as it selects candidates and frames political alternatives. And "within" the elected legislator, it competes with both the constituency and values of the legislator himself for his political attention and loyalty. The representative system by which democracies govern themselves rests squarely on the interaction of legislator, party, and constituency. The study of the parties as electoral organizations must inevitably be a study of this process of representation.[1]

The nature of the political party's role in this representational system has occasioned a major debate within academic political science during the past generation. Proponents of "party responsibility" have suggested that the party's function must be broader than the mere selection of candidates and the election of officeholders. It must, the argument goes, lay down a party program, elect candidates loyal to it, and hold its elected officials accountable for its implementation. Only in this way, they maintain, can the voter be assured that the mandate he approved will be translated into public policy.[2] Granted that the American parties do not now meet these demanding canons of "responsibility," one might ask the more modest question of whether the

1. For a general survey of concepts and definitions of representation, see John A. Fairlie, "The Nature of Political Representation," *American Political Science Review*, XXXIV (1940), Nos. 2 and 3, 236–248, 456–466. For a provocative re-examination of the Burkean dilemmas, see Eulau, Wahlke, Buchanan, and Ferguson, "The Role of the Representative: Some Empirical Observations on the Theory of Edmund Burke," *ibid.*, LIII (1959), No. 3, 742–756.

2. The debate is summarized and analyzed in Austin Ranney, *The Doctrine of Responsible Party Government,* "Its Origins and Present State" (Urbana: University of Illinois Press, 1954).

parties, by controlling the selection of public officials and putting them into their debt, do not eventually ensure some party discipline and cohesion. In other words, do disciplined parties foster party discipline in their chosen and elected candidates? Since these debates largely concern the role of the party within a system of representation, the conclusions of the following chapters touch them very directly.

Probably no one since Edmund Burke has defined the dilemmas of party in the representative process as clearly as he did. Both in his concept of the political party as an organization pursuing the national interest and in his definition of the representative's responsibility to the nation as a whole, Burke attempted to liberate both party and legislator from the local, particular, and even narrowly selfish sources of their political support. Yet, with today's advances in public education and civic participation, in transportation and communication, both party and representative find themselves more than ever thrown back on the local constituency. The interdependence of party, constituency, and legislator was perhaps never greater. Party and legislator, now more than in Burke's time, are chained to Bristol.

The political party and the process of representation, then, form the two main axes of this study. It focuses on those points in the political process at which they intersect. The process of choosing representatives begins months before the direct primary with the first stirrings of political ambition within potential candidates, progresses through the primary and general elections, and continues through the legislative session as the legislator sorts out and resolves competing claims for his loyalties. That process forms the organizational outline of this study. The intervention of party at significant points suggests its major concerns.

Limits of the Study

Even the informed American involves himself in the affairs of state with a high degree of selectivity. The great quadrennial contest for the presidency may catch his fancy, but in the election of a state legislature or the deliberations of the local school board he often is monumentally uninterested. If state and local govern-

4

ment, especially, does not titillate, shock, or frighten, it might as well be taxing Zulus or subdividing Mars as far as he is concerned. Political scientists, unfortunately, have not always been immune to the same fascinations. For years, scholarship in politics or the political process meant study of national politics and national elections. It is no secret that, in the profession of political science, greater status and prestige attached to those who studied national and international political phenomena rather than the supposedly less exciting matters of the states and localities. In fact, the study of state and local government and its politics was assigned a separate area within political science and effectively isolated from the other concerns of the profession.

Recently, scholars of politics have increasingly sought materials for their study in the apparatus and operation of state and local governments.[3] The city council and the state legislature came within their ken, not out of interest in a particular city or state, but as representative and convenient specimens of the legislative process. The events and politics of the localities, the theorists of the political system discovered, offered laboratories for their hypotheses as useful as the arenas of national politics. As a result, the study of state and local politics has focused increasingly on the search for general knowledge of politics rather than on political history, political journalism, or the salty political anecdote.

Unhappily and arbitrarily, the study of the complex of political decisions and actions we so blithely sum up as "the political process" must, of necessity, be static. The scholar must, for a variety of practical reasons, interrupt that flow of political activity at a given point and around that point block out a range of events and data that will be his scholarly province. This study cuts into the politics of one state, Pennsylvania, at one election

3. See, for instance, V.O. Key, Jr., *American State Politics,* "An Introduction" (New York: A.A. Knopf, 1956), and Leon D. Epstein, *Politics in Wisconsin* (Madison: University of Wisconsin Press, 1958). This direction in research has also been fostered by a series of grants for research in state politics by the Committee on Political Behavior of the Social Science Research Council; this study is one they have aided.

of representatives to the lower house of the state legislature, that of November, 1958. These are, however, only the temporal and spatial limits of the data of the study. Its concerns and hypotheses are for political parties, elections, and legislatures in general.

The Pennsylvania House of Representatives of 210 members is, as state lower houses go, a large one. Only four states, all of them in New England, have larger ones. The 210 legislators represent 154 constituencies; of these constituencies, 113 elect one member, thirty-one elect two, five elect three, and five choose four. These 154 constituencies form the basic unit for this study and determine the basic categories of data. Wherever possible and feasible, I have used data for all 154 legislative districts and all 210 legislators, but the limits of time and personnel have forced refuge in some instances in a 50 per-cent sample of the legislative constituencies and candidates.[4]

I am, of course, aware of the possibility, indeed the likelihood, that the special conditions and traditions of Pennsylvania may color the findings. One can only attempt to discover these conditions, articulate them, and make the proper allowances for them. Two characteristics of the state, however, make it an ideal locale for a study such as this. Its diversity offers an almost matchless variety of political environments and data in which to cast hypotheses and generalizations. Second, since Pennsylvania is

4. The specialist is directed to Appendix A, "A Note on Method," for a discussion of the sample and other methodological procedures. The data on which the following is based fall into these main categories: (a) constituency: data on population; urban-rural ratios; religious, racial, and ethnic composition; primary and general election data; social and economic indexes; (b) party: data on party strength, factionalism, recruitment practices, leadership, and attempts to control the nomination process; (c) candidate: data on the social characteristics, political history, candidate recruitment, and legislative attitudes of both victorious and defeated candidates for the legislature; (d) legislator: data on the roll-call behavior, as it indicates issue preferences and party cohesion, of the elected legislators. The particular sources of the various data will, of course, be noted throughout the book. The reader should know here that all of the data on the candidates and the parties and some of that on the constituencies derive from personal interviews with the candidates and with party and community leaders in their districts. The great bulk of the data depend, therefore, on the wisdom and candor of some five hundred politicians and community informants throughout Pennsylvania.

generally acknowledged to have a vigorous party system, one has the advantage of studying there a party apparatus for which the theories of party discipline and responsibility ought to hold true if they do anywhere. Yet, any scholar who attempts to build generalizations about political behavior and political systems must proceed on the conviction that, stripped of provincial and temporal distinctions, one government and its political system retain aspects common and comparable to those of other states, localities, and nations. Without that assumption, there can be no political theory, or even political generalization.

The Setting

Those who know Pennsylvania marvel at its prodigious diversity. A state of mighty industrial centers and urban complexes, over half of its acreage is still in forests. The extremes in wealth and poverty are just as striking; just a few hours' drive from the Main Line suburbs of Philadelphia lie the bitterly depressed mining towns of the Wyoming Valley. Within its boundaries, Yankee and "old settler" families mix with the quaintly provincial "Pennsylvania Dutch" and with the many ethnic and national groups of Southern and Eastern Europe. This diversity is for the scholar both attraction and frustration—attraction in the wide range of social variables it affords him, frustration in the immensely complex and heterogeneous politics in which it results.[5]

The 1950 census ranked Pennsylvania, with its population of 10,498,012, as the third most populous state of the union, and by 1960 it was still the third most populous, with a population of 11,319,366. From 1940 to 1950, the state showed a population

5. The data on Pennsylvania in this chapter are drawn from the 1950 census; Edward F. Cooke and G. Edward Janosik, *Guide to Pennsylvania Politics* (New York: Holt, 1957); Jacob Tanger, Harold Alderfer, and M. Nelson McGeary, *Pennsylvania Government* (Rev. ed.; State College: Penns Valley Press, 1950); Wayland F. Dunaway, *A History of Pennsylvania* (Englewood Cliffs, N.J.: Prentice-Hall, 1948); *The Pennsylvania Manual*, Vol. 94 (Commonwealth of Pennsylvania, 1958); *Pennsylvania Statistical Abstract: 1959* (Department of Internal Affairs, Commonwealth of Pennsylvania); and National Council of the Churches of Christ in the U.S.A., *Churches and Church Membership in the United States*, Series C, Nos. 8 and 9 (1957).

increase of only 6 per cent, in contrast to the 14.5 per-cent increase for the country as a whole; from 1950 to 1960, its population increased only 7.8 per cent, while the national growth percentage was 18.5. This lagging rate of growth, below that of three-fourths of the states, indicates rather strikingly that opportunity for Pennsylvanians often lies outside the boundaries of the state. Pennsylvania remains racially typical of the Northern, urban, industrial states. Over 6 per cent of its population in 1950 and well over 7 per cent in 1960 was nonwhite.

These residents of the state live overwhelmingly in its urban and metropolitan areas; 70.5 per cent in 1950 and 71.6 per cent in 1960 lived in urban places of 2,500 or more. That 1960 percentage made Pennsylvania the seventeenth most urban state. The two great urban centers at each end of the state, Philadelphia and Pittsburgh, dominate the distribution of the state's population. Almost 53 per cent of the people of the state in 1960 lived in those nine Pennsylvania counties of the Philadelphia and Pittsburgh "standard metropolitan areas." [6] In fact, by 1960, 78 per cent of all Pennsylvanians lived in one of the twenty-two (of sixty-seven) Pennsylvania counties the Census Bureau places in a standard metropolitan area.

Something of both the population shifts and urban-rural changes within the state can be pieced together by examining population loss and gain totals for the sixty-seven counties. Whereas the state gained more than a million new faces between 1940 and 1958, the year of this study, twenty-seven counties showed population losses in that period. The most startling losses were generally registered by counties that had been centers of coal-mining. Less dramatic losses occurred in the rural, less prosperous farming counties. The suburban counties ringing the city of Philadelphia showed the greatest population increase in the period. However, most counties with substantial urban centers

6. These "standard metropolitan areas," a new Census Bureau category, comprise those counties that are "essentially metropolitan in character and socially and economically integrated with the central city" (p. xv, Vol. II, Part 38, *1950 Census of Population*). In these two cases, they include Allegheny, Beaver, Westmoreland, and Washington counties in the Pittsburgh area and, in the Philadelphia area, Philadelphia, Bucks, Montgomery, Delaware, and Chester counties.

(say, over 50,000) also marked up small to moderate gains.

Ethnically, Pennsylvania is the American "melting pot" in microcosm, and the triteness of the observation makes it no less true. Even in 1950 there were 776,609 foreign-born residents in the state; in addition, over two million first-generation Americans (of at least one foreign-born parent) were counted. In all, 555,069 Pennsylvanians in 1950 either were born in Italy or had one parent who was born there. Poland, Germany, the USSR, and Eire follow, in that order, as countries of national origin. Though these groups dominate the arrivals of this century, earlier German and Anglo-Saxon groups predominate in many counties of the state. But, beyond the forbidding columns of census data, one need only look at the people and places about him in Pennsylvania to grasp its ethnic diversity. A quick thumbing through the telephone directory of any Pennsylvania city discloses its ethnic heritage, and in most of the cities one still finds thriving ethnic clubs and fraternal groups. In some parts of rural Pennsylvania, it is not uncommon to find a fifth- or sixth-generation Yankee farmer living next to a first-generation farmer of Lithuanian parentage.

What is true about Pennsylvania's ethnic background is also true of its religious traditions. The National Council of Churches' 1957 estimates of church membership in the state show that, among affiliated church membership, 47.9 per cent of Pennsylvanians are Protestant, 46.4 per cent Catholic, and 5.7 per cent Jewish. Reflecting the large population of German origin, the largest single Protestant denomination is the United Lutheran Church, at 26.9 per cent of the Protestants; the Methodists are second, at 18.6 per cent. Of the counties in which the Catholics are estimated to have more than 50 per cent of the church membership, all are either urban-industrial, steel mill, or mining centers. At the other extreme, there are thirty-one counties over 70 per cent Protestant and five in which there is not a single Roman Catholic church. What results, then, is a heavy concentration of Roman Catholics and Jews in the industrial and mining centers in the east and west of the state, leaving an overwhelmingly Protestant belt in the rural, somewhat isolated, central section of the state.

9

The same diversity that marks its people also characterizes the economy of Pennsylvania. Although it is not predominantly an agricultural state (only 2.4 per cent of its residents were farmers or farm managers in 1950), it ranked fourteenth among the states in value of farm products produced. Small, family-sized farms predominate, and the crops are diverse; dairying and truck farming remain especially important, however. Even though many of the farmers of the state till ungrateful and unproductive soil, the state boasts in Lancaster County the richest single (nonirrigated) agricultural county in the United States by value of products. Along with farming, the extractive industries have dominated rural Pennsylvania. Their decline constitutes one of the state's major tragedies and its most serious economic problem. Total production in net tons of anthracite coal is now one-third, and that of bituminous coal now one-half, of what it was in the 1920's. Even between 1956 and 1958, declines in the production of anthracite, bituminous, crude petroleum, clays, sand and gravel, stone, lime, and cement were reported.

Increasingly, therefore, Pennsylvania has within recent years relied on its industrial productivity. Dominating this industrial base is steel. Pennsylvania's steel production capacity is greater than any other state's and by itself accounts for over one-fourth of the total capacity of the entire country. In 1960, state agencies estimated that almost 1,500,000 of its 4,291,000 work force were engaged in manufacturing, 58 per cent of them in durable-goods manufacturing, and 42 per cent in nondurables. Over 500,000 of that total worked in the primary metals or textile and apparel industries.

Unhappily for the state, economic prosperity has been at best spotty over the past decade. As of mid-1960, over 7 per cent of the state's civilian labor force was unemployed; a year earlier, Pennsylvania had shown the highest percentage (8) of insured unemployed in the nation. Certain labor areas within the state have, moreover, fared even worse. Unemployment in 1960 persisted well above the 10 per-cent mark in the Scranton, Wilkes-Barre–Hazelton, and Pottsville labor areas, approaching at times a mark over 15 per cent. A year or two earlier, at the time of this

10

superiority into the 1950's. From 1943 to 1954, they controlled both the governorship and both houses of the state legislature.

In the 1950's, however, the state entered a period of ever intensifying two-party competition. Reform Democrats in 1951 defeated the entrenched Republican organization in Philadelphia, and since then the two metropolitan areas of the state have been Democratic bastions. At the same time, the Republicans began to experience a series of debilitating intraparty squabbles, both over allegiance to national candidates (Eisenhower or Taft) and over control of the state party machinery. The election in 1954 of George Leader, the Democratic gubernatorial candidate, formally signaled the resurgence of the Democrats. In the same election, the Democrats carried the lower house of the state legislature by a modest margin and came within two seats of capturing the Senate, long considered a Republican citadel. In 1956, the Republicans carried the state for Eisenhower and won back the state legislature, but lost a Senate seat to Democrat Joseph Clark. Two years later, the Democrats carried the state for Gov. David L. Lawrence, recaptured the lower house of the legislature, but lost the Senate contest to Republican Hugh Scott. By 1958, then, Pennsylvania found itself the battleground of two closely matched, well-oiled, and well-financed state party organizations.

The trend away from Republican domination of Pennsylvania politics to intense party competition is clearly reflected in party registration totals within the state for the decade of the 1950's. From 1950 to 1954, the Republicans claimed from 58.9 to 59.4 per cent of the two-party registration in the state. In 1956, however, it stood at 54.2 per cent, and by 1960 the Democratic registration moved a scant 2,965 ahead of the Republican. The explanation of this Democratic trend is not a simple one. Most likely, effective Democratic leadership and appealing "new faces," coupled with Republican feuding and ineptness, have made a difference. The Democrats have also belatedly begun to cultivate the urban, industrial, lower-status social and economic groups that Democratic parties in other Northern, urban states do. To put it another way, only since 1950 have the Democrats of Pennsylvania shaken off some of the traditional party appeals and begun

12

to the silk-stocking districts in and around Philadelphia and to the depressed coal fields of Schuylkill County, and the Democrats must woo the conservative farmers of the rural counties as well as the urban proletariat of the Monongahela Valley steel towns. Furthermore, local centers of political power retain impressive strength. Many of the cities, boroughs, and counties retain patronage and elective spoils for local party organizations. Courthouse and city-hall organizations, as a result, flourish famously in the Keystone State. Over and against this decentralization and fragmentation of politics prevails a tradition of strong gubernatorial leadership, enforced by the 50,000 state patronage jobs. Pennsylvania, too, feels the ubiquitous trend to election campaigns centralized around the gubernatorial candidates.

All these political contentions take place in and reflect the Pennsylvania tradition of "strong" politics. Old-style political machines, with their armies of committeemen and party workers, prevail in many small towns and cities, as well as in the metropolitan centers of the state. Even in the predominantly rural sectors of the state, the degree of political activity is surprisingly high, and even here the parties can often turn out an amazingly disciplined vote in the state's closed primary. Throughout the state there reigns, in varying degrees of disguise, a corresponding politics of exploitation. The tradition of politics as a system of immediate and direct rewards lives on and attracts to both party banners workers who openly seek those rewards. It is not at all unusual, for instance, to find virtually the entire top leadership of a county organization holding some elective or appointive public office. For others, such as local contractors, the rewards of political activity may be less public, though equally tangible.

The broader implications of such a tradition of virile, if not virulent, politics are clear. First, only scattered and usually limited antiorganization sentiments exist on which maverick office-seekers can play. The banners of insurgency have not traditionally attracted large followings in Pennsylvania. Second, the tradition of politics as personal gain perforce means that Pennsylvania politics are nonideological and often issueless. One can talk to hundreds of local political leaders in the state without hearing the words "liberal" or "conservative" spoken. In the local political

14

barony in Pennsylvania, the reward system becomes, instead of a means to election success or policy enactment, the political end in itself.

The scholarly literature, of course, conventionally describes American political parties as nonideological, decentralized, pragmatic coalitions of disparate interests. The generalization applies to Pennsylvania, as the previous paragraphs show, with even more than usual accuracy. This is not to argue that one can find no ideological commitments within the Pennsylvania parties, but rather that they exert no particular influence on party policy and strategy. Within the Democratic Party, one can find New and Fair Deal Democrats and an even vaguer ideological allegiance to "the working man." And, within the Republicans there are, too, ideological currents—the "more-business-in-government" and tax-reduction strains, for instance. But they have not created in either party any real programmatic cast. Given their strength and cohesion, especially in state-wide politics and in the state legislature, the Pennsylvania parties are strong and disciplined without achieving any substantial issue or program image.

The Pennsylvania Legislature

Finally, a few words about the Pennsylvania General Assembly are in order. The Senate has a membership of fifty, and the House of Representatives has 210. The members of the House serve for two-year terms and represent a total of 154 election districts. Of these districts, 113 are one-member districts, thirty-one elect two members, five elect three, and five choose four. The Pennsylvania Constitution guarantees that each of the sixty-seven counties, regardless of its population, will have a seat in the House. Aside from the inequalities that such an assurance introduces, the House of Representatives, as the following chapter will indicate, accurately represents the state's population. The most recent reapportionment of the seats of the House was completed in 1953 and reflects the 1950 census data.

Through 1959, the General Assembly met only biennially, but in that year the voters approved a constitutional amendment to begin annual sessions. Accordingly, the legislature raised the $6,000 per term salary of the representatives to a more munificent

$12,000 for the two annual sessions in a term. Observers speculate that the increased salary and heightened responsibilities may alter the recruitment of the representatives, but more of that later. Like most state assemblies, the affairs of the House of Representatives have imposed only a part-time burden on the members, both during the year and during the weeks of the session. It is not unusual for a week's meetings to convene late on Monday afternoon and break up early Wednesday afternoon for the legislators to hurry home to family and business.

Before 1958, the partisan composition of the House of Representatives seesawed between slim majorities of one and then the other party. In 1952 and 1956, Republican majorities controlled the House; in 1954 and 1958, the Democrats organized it. Here in the legislature one finds the same party strength and discipline apparent in the state as a whole; a later chapter will discuss the high degree of party cohesion on House roll-call votes. Party caucuses are a regular, important, and often determining part of the legislative process. The great majority of the 210 legislators are in varying mixtures inexperienced, uninformed, or disinterested and look to party leaders for guidance.

The 1959 session of the House of Representatives ran sporadically from mid-January to early January of 1960. The Democrats controlled the chamber, 108 to 102, ensuring the election of a Democratic speaker and committee chairmen. The governor, David L. Lawrence, was also a Democrat. To keep the constitutional majority of 106 votes present and voting through tax and appropriation bills taxed the party's leadership in the extreme. The need to raise new taxes occasioned the sharpest battle of the session. After protracted debate, the Republicans and a handful of Democrats refused to pass the Governor's tax package and forced the unhappy Democratic majority to accept a 1 per-cent addition (to 4 per cent) to the state sales tax. In fact, in the past few legislative sessions budgetary issues have, not surprisingly, provided the chief political fireworks. The state's depressed economy quite probably intensifies the usually troublesome tax and financial issues.

2 • The Constituencies

The 154 constituencies of the Pennsylvania House of Representatives are the fields on which party and candidate play for public favor. Their widely varying nature influences the party strengths, and their political cultures and expectations define the limits of party activity. Their criteria for political leadership govern the emergence of aspiring office-seekers. Both the party and the legislator must accept the limits which the constituency, directly and indirectly, sets on their operations and activities. The assumptions of representation in a democracy demand as much.

The Reapportionment of 1953

The two houses of the Pennsylvania General Assembly represent both people and acreage. In the upper chamber, the Senate, the constitution forbids the allotment of more than one-sixth (16.7 per cent) of the seats to any one city or county; Philadelphia, with 19.7 per cent of the state's population in 1950, was consequently underrepresented. Otherwise, the inequities which exist in senatorial apportionment are the work of the two houses.[1]

"People" as the criterion for apportionment fares better in the constitutional section dealing with the House of Representatives. Article II, Section 17, typical of the entire constitution in its detail, provides that:

> The members of the House of Representatives shall be apportioned among the several counties on a ratio obtained by dividing the population of the State as ascertained by the most recent United States census by two hundred. Every county containing less than five ratios shall have one representative for every full ratio, and an additional representative when the surplus exceeds half a ratio; but each county shall have at least one representative. Every county containing five ratios or more shall have one representative for every full ratio. Every city containing a population equal to a ratio shall elect separately its proportion of the representatives allotted to the county in which it is located. Every city entitled to more than four representatives, and every county having over one hundred thousand inhabitants, shall be divided into districts of compact and contiguous territory, each district to elect its proportion of representatives according to its population, but no district shall elect more than four representatives.

Under these provisions, the legislature in 1953 worked out the present allotment of 210 House seats to 154 constituencies—113 one-member and forty-one multimember districts.

If one divides the 1950 Pennsylvania population of 10,498,012 by 200, a "ratio" (as defined by the constitution) of 52,490 results. A total of twenty-seven of the state's sixty-seven counties had populations in 1950 below the 52,490 figure; sixteen of the twenty-seven, in fact, totaled fewer than 35,000 residents. The constitution guarantees the right of all twenty-seven to a seat apiece, thereby producing the major source of unequal apportionment. For the thirty-four counties with between one and five ratios

1. Article II, Section 16. For a report on apportionment in the Pennsylvania Senate, see Lee E. Corter, "Pennsylvania Ponders Apportionment," *Temple Law Quarterly*, XXXII (1959), No. 3, 279–294.

sity that result from the state's population distribution are even more dramatic. Twelve of the state's districts, all of them in Philadelphia, have population densities greater than 30,000 people per square mile, with a top of 69,954 per square mile in Philadelphia's Eleventh District. Yet thirty-four of the 154 have fewer than a hundred souls per square mile, and a cumulative total of eighty-five average fewer than a thousand. The wooded expanses of Forest County contain only 11.8 per square mile. These extremes of population density are not without political importance—campaigning and contacts with constituents, for instance, vary greatly between the Philadelphia districts and those in Lycoming, Forest, and the other sparsely settled counties.

All population data thus far employed have been those of the 1950 census, on which the 1953 apportionment was based. Reports from the count of 1960 indicate that, as one would suspect, not all of Pennsylvania increased in population at the 7.8 per-cent rate of the state as a whole. The trends of the 1940's generally continued into the 1950's—the coal and forest areas lost the greatest population. Greene and Schuykill counties, both coal-mining regions, suffered the greatest losses (more than 13 per-cent decline), with three other coal counties (Fayette, Northumberland, and Luzerne) not far behind. The suburban counties around Philadelphia were the chief gainers; the four counties encircling Philadelphia and included in the Philadelphia standard metropolitan area (Bucks, Chester, Delaware, and Montgomery) experienced a 48.4 per-cent increase in population between 1950 and 1960; their share of the state's population accordingly rose from 10.2 to 14.0 per cent. On the whole, however, the population gain of Philadelphia suburbia and that of Cumberland County (Harrisburg suburbia) were the only dramatic ones within the state. They were, at least, the only counties that added more than 25 per cent to their 1950 populations.

To look into 1960 data a little further, the latest state population total, if divided by 200, would produce an apportionment ratio of 56,597; thirty counties (as against twenty-seven by 1950 data) would fall below ratio size and be to some degree overrepresented. And fourteen (as opposed to the earlier sixteen) re-

20

main below 35,000 in population. The seven counties with populations over the five-ratio mark of 282,985 (Allegheny, Bucks, Delaware, Luzerne, Montgomery, Philadelphia, and Westmoreland) account for 50.4 per cent of the state's total now, but hold 45.2 per cent of the House seats. The four counties around Philadelphia, though, with their present 14 per cent of the population, have only 9 per cent of the seats. Despite these inequities, one may venture the guess that the passage of ten years worked less drastic distortions in the Pennsylvania apportionment than in those of many states.

Constitutional mandate rather than legislative willfulness, therefore, prevents equality of representation in the lower chamber. Except for the constitutional insistence that every county, no matter how lightly populated, be given a seat, the House of Representatives in 1953 represented the state's population in about as equitable an apportionment as legislative ingenuity and partisan forbearance could devise. The problem of constitutionally imposed inequalities, however, is not peculiar to Pennsylvania; only twelve states are free of such constitutional limitations.[4] Nor are the Pennsylvania strictures as demanding as those of many other states. It, at least, has no maximum limits, no regressive representational scales, no county-unit provisions. Yet, as modest as the guarantee of a seat per county may be, its justification is now less apparent than it was in 1872. The counties of the state may have constituted genuine communities some eighty or ninety years ago, but revolutions in transportation, communication, and the economy have changed that. Especially in those less populous counties that benefit from the guarantee of a legislative district, it is not unusual for many county residents to work, shop, and play outside the county. The 10,387 residents of Fulton County on the state's southern border, for instance, increasingly find work in nearby counties or in Maryland. A considerable number make the sixty-four–mile round trip every day to Hagerstown, Maryland, for work or less frequently for shopping or entertain-

4. Gordon E. Baker, *Rural versus Urban Political Power* (Garden City, New York: Doubleday, 1955), p. 12.

21

ment. If the county was once a self-contained political unit, it seems to be one no longer.

Who Gets Represented?

Political coalitions and interests are often so finely balanced that even the smallest over- or underrepresentation may tip the scales of political power. In the 1959 session of the House, Republicans held twelve of the thirteen seats in the least populous counties of the state. In the preceding session, the Republicans likewise held twelve of the thirteen. Of the districts with populations above 50,000, the Democrats in 1958 won fifty, the Republicans won thirty, and the parties split two. In a chamber closely divided between 108 Democrats and 102 Republicans, skewed representation of this sort deprived the Democrats of a badly needed working majority.

In addition to the overrepresentation of a political party, important social and economic interests within the population may be overrepresented as well. Most of the disparity in the representation of social and economic groupings bears some relation to urban or rural residence. Negroes, for instance, few of whom live in rural areas, gained nothing from the overrepresentation of less populous counties. None of the twenty districts in the state in which Negroes comprised 10 or more per cent of the population had fewer than 40,000 people per legislator. Nor did middle- or upper-income groups in the state share in the overrepresentation given the underpopulated counties. None of the thirty-seven districts with the greatest percentages of people earning $5,000 or more a year had fewer than 40,000 people.

Not surprisingly, the distribution of occupational groups by population of district shows the farmers to be overrepresented in the House. Thirty of the thirty-eight constituencies with the greatest percentage of farmers fell below the 50,000 population mark and, therefore, below the median population per legislator. Conversely, the districts with the lowest concentration of white collar workers (clerical and sales) were the least populous districts. The distribution of the professional-managerial and "blue collar" groups is less clear-cut, perhaps reflecting the changing economies

22

of the low-population counties. Often heavily forested and plagued with marginal farm lands, they have been losing their workers to nearby industrial centers or enticing small industry into the county.

All these disparities may be more neatly explained by examining the way in which the constituencies of the House represented the urban-rural structure of the state in 1953. Political scientists have for years been engaged in precisely this type of analysis, finding, with almost monotonous regularity, that, as a group, the state legislatures scandalously overrepresent rural America. The most notable recent example of this scholarly genre, Gordon Baker's study,[5] finds that only two states accord urban areas representation "equal" to that given rural areas. Seven more, including Pennsylvania, only "moderately" underrepresent the urban areas.[6] His judgment rests only on the representation given Allegheny (Pittsburgh) and Philadelphia counties, however.

If one breaks the Pennsylvania districts into a number of urban categories, it becomes clear that Baker's conclusion holds true for all the cities of the state. In Table 1, all of the districts have been put in one of three groups depending on whether a majority of their populations live in cities over 100,000, in any combination of urbanized area or urban place from 2,500 to 100,000, or in rural places.[7] The districts of lowest population emerge quite naturally as those in which half or more of the population lives in rural areas. But, contrary to what one finds in many states, the "big-city" districts of Pittsburgh and Philadelphia suffer no more underrepresentation than do those of smaller towns and cities. Only those groups of districts in which a majority of the residents live in rural areas or in urban places of less than 10,000 population are overrepresented.

5. *Ibid.*
6. *Ibid.*, pp. 12 f.
7. I have adopted the Census Bureau's population figure of 2,500 as the dividing point between "urban" and "rural" more out of convenience than conviction. The term "urbanized area" is also used here in the definition of the Census Bureau: one or more central cities of at least 50,000 inhabitants, plus closely settled incorporated places and unincorporated areas that comprise its urban fringe.

23

When one examines the cities themselves, the same conclusions emerge. Pittsburgh and Philadelphia, with a combined
population of 2,748,411 and 26.2 per cent of the state's 1950 population, received 24.8 per cent of the representatives.[8] If one takes
the eleven other Pennsylvania cities with populations over 50,000

TABLE 1

URBAN-RURAL NATURE OF THE CONSTITUENCIES
BY POPULATION

Population per legislator in district	Districts classified by majority of population living in:		
	Cities over 100,000 (N = 49)	Urban places (2,500–100,000) and/or urbanized areas (N = 46)	Rural areas (N = 59)
	Percentage		
0– 9,999	0	2.2	5.1
10–19,999	0	0	8.5
20–29,999	0	0	6.8
30–39,999	0	4.3	11.9
40–49,999	32.7	21.7	40.7
50–59,999	38.8	43.5	20.3
60–69,999	24.5	26.1	3.4
70–79,999	4.1	2.2	3.4
Totals	100.1	100.0	100.1

and from which whole legislative districts have been carved,[9] he
finds that they house 9.1 per cent of the people of the state, but
were given only 8.1 per cent of its legislative seats. For inequities

8. The seat total of thirteen for Pittsburgh includes one representative
elected also by the borough of Mt. Oliver, population: 6,646.
9. These are Allentown, Altoona, Bethlehem (that part of the city in
Northampton County), Erie, Harrisburg, Johnstown, Lancaster, Reading,
Scranton, Wilkes-Barre, and York. The Johnstown district also includes the
adjacent borough of Dale, which has a population of 3,310.

24

of this size, perhaps "slight" underrepresentation would be closer to the truth of the matter than "moderate."

By 1960, as earlier data suggest, Pennsylvania cities had joined cities throughout the country in recording population losses. Philadelphia and Pittsburgh, at 23.0 per cent of the population, were by 1960 overrepresented in the House (with 24.8 per cent of the seats), and so were the eleven cities over 50,000 and constituting legislative districts (7.9 per cent of population and 8.1 per cent of seats). As the discussion a few pages earlier suggests, the growing suburban areas suffer the greatest underrepresentation at present, and the declining rural areas the greatest overrepresentation. The tides of urban migration have at the same time eased the inequities the older center cities suffered so long.

Although these 1960 census data indicate the direction of the trends at work at the time of this study, the main bulk of the census data used is still that of the 1950 enumeration. A word of justification may be in order for that reliance. The great value of the population characteristics of the constituencies—both the absolute numbers and the urban-rural and socioeconomic data— lies in the fact that these populations shaped the political processes at work in the 1958 legislative elections. For an assessment of their interaction with the parties and candidates in the 1950's, then, the data of 1950 are certainly at least as relevant as those of 1960.

Multimember Districts

It has recently come to the attention of American political scientists that multimember districts in the states are vastly more common than they had suspected.[10] Multimember districts elect about 45 per cent of all the legislators in state lower chambers, and, if one counts only the states with plural districts, the percentage rises to 58. In Pennsylvania, 97 of the 210 representatives (46 per cent) are chosen from two-, three-, or four-member districts.

10. See Maurice Klain, "A New Look at the Constituencies: The Need for a Recount and a Reappraisal," *American Political Science Review*, XLIX (1955), No. 4, 1105–1119.

The multimember districts bunch much more closely around the median population per district than do the single-member districts. None of them in 1950 had less than 30,000 people per legislator or more than 70,000, and thirty of the forty-one fell between 40,000 and 60,000. Furthermore, the multimember districts tended to include higher income levels and higher concentrations of professional, technical, managerial, and white collar occupational groups than did the single-member constituencies. Conversely, they had fewer farmers and farm managers. These tendencies of the multimember districts result from two factors. Very simply, the creation of multimember districts in the less populous rural areas is arithmetically impossible. That fact alone biases the distribution of the single- and multimember constituencies. But the income and occupational character of the multimember districts also reflect their location in suburban and urban areas.[11] These tendencies appear especially marked in the four-member districts. These five districts were all fashioned from the suburban and urban fringe areas of Pittsburgh and Philadelphia. By contrast, the three-member districts are a mixed lot: one in urban Philadelphia, one in agricultural Lancaster County, and the other three in counties (Fayette, Cambria, and Northampton) dotted with many and diverse mill and mining towns.

The impact and effect of these multimember constituencies on the representational system of the House is not easily assessed. There has certainly been no breakdown in the two-party system of the sort that some scholars predict as the price of multimember districting. No third parties have sprung into existence, and it is unlikely they will as long as the multiple districts are not coupled with some form of proportional representation. In fact, little representation of even the minority party has occurred.

11. There is a high incidence of multimember districts in the areas combining urbanized areas and urban places between 2,500 and 100,000. This presence of multimember districts in urban areas would tend to confirm Klain's observation (*op. cit.*, p. 1117) that rural interests "almost always spearhead" the drive for single-member districts and that urban elements resist them. In Pennsylvania, however, one would have to cite many exceptions to the rule.

26

In 1958, the majority party carried all but three of the forty-one multimember districts; in other words, the parties split only two two-member districts, and the Republicans took one seat of a four-member district in which the Democrats won three. However, they split no districts in 1956 and only one in 1954.[12]

These sweeps of all the seats of a district bespeak a high degree of party cohesion in the voting. In 1958, a range of less than 5 per cent covered all the candidates of fifty-four of the eighty-two parties running candidates in the multimember elections (two parties each in forty-one elections).[13] And in only eleven did the range extend beyond 10 per cent. In 1956, a total of sixty-five of the eighty-two party tickets showed a deviation of less than five per cent, with only three beyond the 10 per-cent mark.[14] Perhaps in that year the pull of a presidential election imposed greater cohesion on party voting than did the gubernatorial race of 1958.

In the Keystone State, therefore, party cohesion remains too strong to permit the minority party to elect even a single man in these districts. It also remains great enough to balk the possibility of plurality elections. Through a combination of either party-splitting (voting, say, for a Democrat and a Republican in a two-member district) and casting less than a full vote (voting for only one candidate in a two-member district, for instance) it would be possible to elect candidates with less than a majority vote. But such instances are rare. Only once since the 1953 apportionment has a candidate been elected in a multiple-member district

12. This figure is lower than that which Ward reports for multimember elections in Canada, where eight of sixty-two two-member districts for Parliament split over a period of some time. Norman Ward, "Voting in Canadian Two-Member Constituencies," *Public Affairs*, IX (1946), No. 3, 220–223.

13. The range was computed by dividing the difference between the percentage of the vote won by the lowest and the highest candidates by the percentage of the vote won by the lowest candidate.

14. Again, this total is lower than Ward, *op. cit.*, reports from the Canadian experience with two-member districts. In the Canadian districts, the range of vote percentage went above the 5 per-cent mark in twenty-eight of 124 cases.

with less than a majority vote.[15] The Eisenhower landslide of
1956 carried into office a Republican from Northampton County
with a 49.4 per-cent vote. Clearly, then, a strong party system
capable of maintaining cohesive voting for its candidates in multimember districts—and Pennsylvania appears to have it—can fore-
stall the representational quirks and distortions that these districts might otherwise introduce.

Yet, the possibility remains that multimember districts may,
by denying the minority party representation over a fairly large
area, retard the development of competitive two-party politics.
In substance, the multimember district may be a "silent gerrymander" in which the majority party's votes over a diverse area
are so pooled as to deprive the minority party any chance of winning office. Is this, then, a purpose of the multimember districts
in Pennsylvania? What, indeed, is their purpose? Article II, Section 17, of the constitution approves, but in no sense requires, the
creation of multimember districts. The state might conceivably
have been districted into 210 single-member districts in 1953. No
abstract theories of representation explain them; there has been
no overt effort in Pennsylvania to use them to achieve any such
representational goals as minority representation.[16] The multimember districts appear chiefly because they simplify the tangled
mathematics of apportionment. The legislature can ease the
problem of drawing district lines in any apportionment by drawing none. Especially in the event of a county's gaining a seat,
a multimember district permits the addition of a legislator with
minimal disturbance of the present districts. If these multimem-

15. The "majority" figure for the candidates in multimember districts
was obtained by multiplying the candidate's percentage of the total vote by
the number of legislators elected from the district. It is also worth noting
that, since 1953, two candidates have lost elections to the House while
getting a "majority" of votes. In these elections, more candidates received
"majorities" than were to be elected from the district.

16. In Illinois, by contrast, the creation of multimember districts and
a cumulative voting system grew, at least in part, out of a desire to ensure
minority party representation. See George Blair, *Cumulative Voting* (Urbana: University of Illinois Press, 1960).

28

ber constituencies also exist for partisan advantage, that purpose should be disclosed in the following discussion of gerrymandering.

When Is a Gerrymander?

For the question "what is a gerrymander?" political science has a generally accepted answer. V.O. Key, for instance, defines it as "the deliberate formation of legislative districts in such a way as to gain partisan advantage in the composition of the representative body." [17] But the question *"when* is a gerrymander?" is quite another matter. Obviously, the partisans of the major parties are not distributed evenly over the state, and any drawing of district lines will inevitably create some large and wasteful majorities for one party or the other. Just as surely, it will often be impossible—even when the legislative spirit is willing—to permit pockets of party strength to carry even occasional districts. How, then, does one discover a systematic and calculated attempt to dissipate or minimize the partisan strength of the other party?

Take for example Northumberland County in the central part of the state. It has been divided into two districts. The First is a slender, finger-shaped district encompassing the coal-mining area of the county; the Second, composed of the irregularly shaped remainder of the county, is largely agricultural. The districts were possibly so drawn to guarantee the Republicans a safe seat in the second district; the partisan distribution of the county in 1952 suggests that strong possibility. Yet, both districts are reasonably contiguous, and each represents a distinct community, with a homogeneous economy and way of life that contrast sharply with those in the other district. What may seem a gerrymander, albeit of the "small-potatoes" variety, may in fact be a genuine attempt to represent the two communities within the county. Without access to the most private thoughts and hagglings of the men who divided Northumberland County, who is to say that this is or is not a gerrymander?

17. V.O. Key, Jr., *Politics, Parties and Pressure Groups,* (Fourth ed.; New York: Crowell, 1958), p. 332.

One can, of course, look for the grosser signs of gerrymandering among the constituencies. One of the surest telltale marks—the one that gave rise to the very name "gerrymander"—is the wildly eccentric shape of the district. The Fifth District of Lackawanna County resembles an improbable horseshoe, and local politicos testify that it was an attempt to collect all the rural Republican areas of the county into one sure Republican district. But one finds few of these districts in Pennsylvania. Another likely symptom of the gerrymander, the minor tinkerings with district lines from one apportionment to another, leads to other cases. The legislature in 1953 removed the Democratic borough of Duryea from the Sixth District of Luzerne County; whatever the intent, the result was to make the district a bit more secure for the GOP. Also, the Republican vote in the Second District of Montgomery County was bolstered by the addition of two Republican townships in the 1953 districting. (Needless to say, the Republicans controlled the 1953 Pennsylvania legislature.) Illustrations beyond these do not abound. The grosser, easily detectable forms of gerrymandering are simply not apparent in the work of the 1953 legislature.[18]

Until we develop operational definitions of gerrymandering, no firmer conclusions than these can be reached. Common criteria for fair districting often conflict; the standard of territorial compactness may inhibit the attempt to meet another criterion, the representation of homogeneous communities. The additional attempt to represent significant concentrations of party strength may further complicate the decision. Beyond these ambiguities which complicate the identification of a gerrymander, we recognize the universal tendency of party majorities to protect their parties' interests as they go through the toils of districting. It would be naïve and unreasonable to expect them to do otherwise. Obviously, majority parties steal little advantages here and there which hardly meet the general notions of gerrymandering. The

18. A third indication of the gerrymander, great differences in population per district, leads nowhere in Pennsylvania; what fluctations there are can be accounted for on other grounds.

point at which minor peccadilloes become electoral sins is the question.

Multimember districts may, however, be employed as silent and subtle gerrymanders. They afford a way of swallowing up the pockets of strength of the opposing party. Before 1953, Schuylkill County, a coal county in the east-central section of the state, had five one-member districts, four of which elected Republicans. The loss of a seat in the 1953 reapportionment forced a redrawing of district lines. Intsead of creating four one-member districts, the legislature constructed two two-member districts, both of which the Republicans swept in 1954. The Democratic precincts of Frackville and Shenandoah, the backbone of the one Democratic district, were diluted in the two-member districts. Regardless of plan and intent, the effect of the resort to multimember districts clearly resulted in a gerrymandering out of Democratic power. Though such instances are not plentiful and though multimember districts may make population equality more feasible,[19] they can obliterate the strength of the minority party.

Great credit for this low incidence of grossly partisan districting in Pennsylvania belongs to Article II, Section 17, of the Pennsylvania constitution. It simply does not give the legislature much chance for "hanky-panky" in drawing district boundaries. In the first place, forty-one of the 154 constituencies drawn in 1953 were in effect drawn by the constitution. They included the counties given one seat, the cities awarded a seat, and the residue of the counties having one seat after its major city was given its seat or seats. Civil boundaries define these districts, and the 1953 legislature could exercise no discretion here. Second, the constitution demands that cities over "ratio" size be treated as separate districts and thereby thwarts any legislative desire to carve up and distribute the urban vote. Aside from those cities getting one seat, six got two seats,[20] leaving the legislators only the narrow alternatives of making the city a two-member district

19. Klain, *op. cit.*, p. 1117.
20. Allentown, Altoona, Erie, Harrisburg, Reading, and Scranton.

or dividing it. And the practical necessity of following ward lines narrows this area of discretion even more. The constitution also provides that two-seat counties with over 100,000 population must be districted into two one-member districts, leaving the legislature only the decision over where to draw the dividing line.

In addition to the control imposed by the constitution, a second check results from the increasing homogeneity of many areas of the state. As upper- and upper-middle income groups flee to the suburbs, Philadelphia and Pittsburgh, for example, become more homogeneously Democratic. Fewer chances to gerrymander a minority party in or out occur when the minority leaves. Or consider the residue of Lancaster County, that part of the county outside the city of Lancaster. Primarily rich farming land of the Pennsylvania Dutch, it is now a three-member district and unfailingly votes Republican. Not even the most determinedly Democratic legislature could carve a Democratic district out of it.

Some credit for this agreeable system of representation goes to the 1953 legislature, of course. Without its willingness to undertake reapportionment, nothing—not even a constitution—could prevail. But major credit must redound to the state's constitution. Even though it is fashionable to berate detailed, lengthy, and painfully explicit state constitutions like Pennsylvania's, the very detail of Article II, Section 17, guarantees legislative districts of generally equal population. Furthermore, its detail to some extent frustrates the would-be gerrymanderers. In view of the failings of mortal legislators in reapportioning their own political bailiwicks, the case for constitutional detail and rigidity on this subject is an impressive one.

Party Loyalties in the Constituencies

In a state as large, populous, and diverse as Pennsylvania, one can find most of the groups that comprise the national coalitions of the two major parties. And, since the 154 legislative constituencies are generally compact and homogeneous, they reflect clearly the pattern of strength of the parties in the state. Of course, in discussing the partisan preferences of the constituencies, one faces a problem of definition. Just which body of Democratic and Republican voters does he measure—those who register with the two parties, those who vote for their presidential or gubernatorial candidates, or those who vote for some local official? The decision here to define the voter loyalties as those expressed in the legislative elections of 1958 grows out of, and is to a large measure dictated by, the focus of this study.

The Rooseveltian revolution in the party alignments of the national parties fairly well by-passed Pennsylvania for twenty years. While the national Democratic Party was becoming, in the conventional oversimplification, the party of urban dwellers, blue collar workers, lower social and economic strata, marginal farmers, and racial and ethnic minorities, the Pennsylvania Republican Party skillfully managed to isolate the state from any such realignment. Through a shrewd use of its entrenched political power and patronage, the Republicans continued through the 1930's and 1940's to hold their superiority in a state that any outsider might reasonably have expected to be a competitive, two-party state. Even as late as 1950, Philadelphia, the state's largest city, was still Republican territory. But Pennsylvania could not forever be quarantined from political change. By the 1950's, the Democrats in the state were recruiting the groups on which the national Democratic Party had earlier built. Philadelphia fell to the Democrats in 1951 and now ranks as a Democratic stronghold along with its sister metropolis, Pittsburgh. By the 1958 legislative elections, party alignment in Pennsylvania reflected national party lines to a great degree.

To a considerable extent, rural-urban differences define the Democratic and Republican constituencies in Pennsylvania. The Republicans dominate the heavily rural districts, and the Democrats enjoy similar superiority in the urban ones. Such a simply urban-rural dichotomy, however, obscures great and important variations in "urbanness." If Philadelphia (population: 2,014,000) and Parkesburg (population: 2,611) are not to be lumped together as "urban," a more discriminating set of categories is essential. Though the Democrats dominate the metropolises of the state, they divide the other urban and urbanized areas with the Republicans (Table 2). Unlike a state such as Wisconsin, however, the

33

Republicans do not dominate the small- and medium-sized cities.[21] Pennsylvania cities of that size, often mill towns or economic centers in the coal fields, appear to have greater Democratic

---

TABLE 2

RELATION BETWEEN PARTY OF LEGISLATOR, PERCENTAGE
VOTE OF DEMOCRATS, AND URBAN-RURAL
CHARACTER OF DISTRICT

	50 per cent or more of population living in:				
	Urban places (100,000 and over) (N = 49)	Urban places (10,000 to 100,000) (N = 15)	Urban places (2,500– 10,000) (N = 7)	Urbanized areas and/ or urban places * (N = 24)	Rural areas (N = 59)
	Percentage				
Party of legislator					
Democrats	87.8	46.7	57.1	50.0	28.8
Republicans	10.2	53.3	42.9	45.8	71.2
Split	2.0	0	0	4.2	0
Percentage vote of Democrats					
Under 40	0	0	0	16.7	28.8
40–44.9	4.1	20.0	14.3	16.7	16.9
45–49.9	6.1	33.3	28.6	12.5	23.7
50–54.9	10.2	0	42.9	16.7	18.6
55–59.9	16.3	33.3	0	12.5	3.4
Over 60	63.3	13.3	14.3	25.0	8.5

* These are districts in which a majority of the residents live in urbanized areas around a center city of 50,000 or more or in a combination of urbanized area and urban places with a population between 2,500 and 100,000.

---

strength. The overpowering Democratic strength in the urban centers with populations over 100,000 is especially evident, not only in number of seats won but in the lavish margins with which

21. Leon D. Epstein, *Politics in Wisconsin* (Madison: University of Wisconsin Press, 1958), Chapter 4. Epstein, however, makes it clear that the special urban character of Wisconsin puts great emphasis on its small and medium cities.

they were won. The corresponding Republican strength in the rural quarters of the state is likewise evident.

Yet, urban-rural differences alone do not account for the differences in Democratic and Republican voter strength. Both parties elect members from both urban and rural constituencies, and from a variety of both urban and rural constituencies at that. When one divides the state by income distribution, however, no significant correlation appears.[22] In fact, the median percentage of population earning $5,000 a year in the Republican districts is, contrary to what one might expect, lower than that for the Democrats.[23] That fact results from Republican domination of low-income rural districts. Income and price levels vary too greatly from the metropolitan areas of the state to the isolated rural areas to be of much use in analysis. The unavailability of data in key areas also seriously compromises the usefulness of occupational data. If, however, one examines somewhat impressionistically the economies of the districts in the various urban and rural categories, the lines of party allegiance begin to emerge.

In districts in which 50 per cent or more of the people live in cities of more than 100,000,[24] income differences appear to be significant. Although the small number of Republican districts (five) will hardly bear much interpretation, they do represent higher income groups. Only eleven of the thirty-six Democratic districts (for which data are available)[25] in these cities have over 18 per cent of the populace earning income over $5,000, but all five of the Republican districts stand above that mark. Furthermore, the Republican districts also prove to be the districts of

22. The coefficient of correlation for the Democratic vote percentage and the percentage of wage earners earning over $5,000 a year is +.087.

23. The median percentage earning more than $5,000 a year in sixty-nine Republican districts is 10.9 and 15.4 for the fifty-two Democratic districts. The other forty-three districts include two which the parties split and forty-one on which there is no income information.

24. Actually, in all these districts, 100 per cent of the people live in cities of more than 100,000.

25. The reader must always bear in mind that census data on occupations and income levels are simply unavailable for many constituencies. This data is reported by urban places, counties, and census tracts and can be translated to legislative districts only for those constituencies following the lines of the civil divisions.

greater concentration of sales, clerical, professional, and managerial groups. For instance, the median percentage of professional and managerial workers in the Democratic districts lies at 12.6, but the Republican district median is 27.3 per cent.[26]

Since thirteen of the fourteen districts having more than 15 per cent Negroes at the 1950 census count fall into this group of districts, their distribution between the parties is important. All of these thirteen heavily Negro districts elected Democratic legislators in 1958. The two major parties, then, divide the metropolitan districts in Pennsylvania along the rather predictable lines of the national party coalitions, the Republicans tending to win only those districts of high income and white collar and managerial occupational groups.

Unhappily, no such tidy division prevails in the districts of medium-city and small-town Pennsylvania. If one combines all the districts in which more than half the residents live in urban places of less than 100,000 or in urbanized areas,[27] he finds that the parties split the forty-six districts almost in half. In 1958, the Democrats won twenty-three, the Republicans twenty-two, and they split one two-member district. To further complicate the problem, income and occupational data are too spotty and incomplete for these constituencies to bear statistical analysis. It remains, therefore, to turn to more casual data.

Of the twenty-three Democratic districts in this category, fully sixteen are heavily laden with either mill or mining towns. Most either line the river valleys that radiate outward from Pittsburgh[28] or cluster along the coal fields of the Wyoming Valley.[29]

26. Compare this data with Andrew R. Baggeley, "White Collar Employment and Republican Vote," *Public Opinion Quarterly*, XX (1956), No. 2, 471–473. Baggeley finds that, in Milwaukee, Wisconsin, income is a less valuable indicator of partisan vote than is occupation; he shows a correlation of $r = +.95$ between percentage Republican vote in the 1954 gubernatorial election and the percentage of white collar workers (professional, managerial, sales, clerical).

27. Columns two, three, and four of Table 2.

28. Allegheny Thirteen and Fourteen; Beaver One and Two; Washington Two; and Westmoreland Two and Three.

29. Lackawanna Three and Four; Luzerne Two, Three, Five, and Six; and Northumberland One.

The final two include mine-rich Carbon County and the Second District of Bucks County, embracing Bristol, Fairless Hills, and Levittown. Aside from these sixteen districts, Democrats also represent districts that are the industrial boroughs and cities that form an indistinguishable part of the Pittsburgh metropolitan complex. The final two Democratic districts defy pigeonholing. The Elk County district contains no urban centers of any size, but the omnibus Second District of Northampton County includes such industrial centers as Easton and Northampton. In these districts, therefore, the Democratic districts predominate in the larger central cities, and especially in the outlying centers of the coal and steel industry.

Quite another matter are the twenty-two Republican constituencies in this same urban category. Eight of the twenty-two constitute what might fairly be called "suburban" districts that encircle Pittsburgh and Philadelphia.[30] These districts are, of course, not without some industrial or commercial activity, but all contain sizable residential areas fashionably distant from the cities in which most of their residents work. Another nine of these Republican districts are mixed urban-rural, most of them containing one or two urban centers surrounded by forested or farm lands.[31] None of the nine represent coal or steel territory, although two contain the major nonmining areas in the heavily mined counties of Lackawanna and Luzerne. Finally, the Republicans represent the districts that are, or are largely, the cities of Altoona, Harrisburg, Lancaster, Wilkes-Barre, and Williamsport. Of these districts, one can only say that they are bastions of the old Republican power in Pennsylvania and reminders of a day when the Republicans carried urban Pennsylvania as certainly as its rural counties. Two of them were in 1958 bases of especially potent Republican machines—the M. Harvey Taylor organization in Harrisburg and Dauphin County and the Republican city machine of Wilkes-Barre.

30. Allegheny Fifteen and Seventeen; Delaware One, Two, and Three; and Montgomery One, Two, and Three.
31. Berks Two, Cameron, Dauphin Two, Lackawanna Five, Lebanon, Luzerne One, Mercer One, Northumberland Two, and Venango.

Let us consider, finally, the fifty-nine districts in which more than half the population lives in rural areas. Here too, income and occupational data, especially on the Democratic constituencies, are available in so few cases as to rule out any systematic analysis with it. Their very absence, however, offers a clue to their significance. Why should such data be available for only five of the seventeen Democratic rural districts but for forty of the forty-two Republican ones? Largely because the Democratic districts are located in larger, multidistrict rural counties, whereas the Republicans win in less populous, one-district counties where census data, available by county, are thereby available by legislative district. A detailed breakdown of the districts amplifies and expands this distinction.

Of course, the fact that only seventeen of the fifty-nine predominantly rural districts are Democratic reveals something in itself. Rural Pennsylvania, especially the relatively unpopulated rural counties, remains, the bulwark of the Republicans. The Republican counties of the center and of the northern and southern tiers of the state stand out on a map like a great, squat "I." Five of the six completely rural districts are Republican, as are eleven of the twelve districts with populations under 30,000. In general, the Republican districts coincide with the farm and forest districts, with the sectors of the state only lightly touched by industrialism, and with a few unincorporated suburban areas. There are a few exceptions,[32] but only a few.

On the other hand, eight of the seventeen Democratic rural districts have strong coal-steel connections.[33] Of the remaining nine districts, five come from the traditional Democratic rural areas of Berks and York counties. Knowledgeable natives trace the Democratic allegiances there to the vestigial liberalism and traditional Democracy of the German immigrants. The remaining four are prevailingly rural,[34] and the explanation of their allegiances lies embedded in layers of local tradition. Even the ac-

32. The second districts of Blair, Mercer, and Schuylkill.
33. Cambria Two, Clearfield One, Fayette One and Two, Green, Luzerne Four, Washington One, and Westmoreland One.
34. Clearfield Two, Fulton, Lycoming Two, and Monroe.

knowledged keepers of local history and folklore falter in analysis. More than one resident of Monroe County, for instance, attributes that county's Democratic leanings to the flight of Southern sympathizers and "draft dodgers" to its hills during the Civil War.

Additional data on the ethnic and religious compositions of the districts throw revealing, if tantalizingly uncertain, light on these partisan alignments. In the absence of any census (or other) data on the ethnic or religious composition of the populations of the districts, we attempted in interviews and observations in the constituencies of the 50 per-cent sample to place each district in simple classifications that would identify its predominant ethnic and religious groups. The results (Table 3), impressionistic though

TABLE 3

RELATION BETWEEN PARTY OF LEGISLATOR (1958) AND ETHNIC AND RELIGIOUS COMPOSITION OF DISTRICT

Party of legislator	Ethnic and national origin *		Religion*	
	N and NE Europe (N = 47)	S and SE Europe; Ireland; Negroes (N = 31)	Protestant (N = 47)	Catholic or evenly divided (N = 31)
	Percentage			
Democrat	34.0	83.9	34.0	83.9
Republican	63.8	16.1	63.8	16.1
Split	2.1	0	2.1	0
Totals	99.9	100.0	99.9	100.0

* Even though the percentages for the two sets of categories are identical, they do not contain exactly the same districts. Needless to say, however, there is considerable overlap; the Northern and Northeastern European national groups tend to be Protestant, for example.

they may be, confirm the conclusions of the last few pages. The Democrats dominate the Southern and Eastern European, Irish, Catholic districts, which are, of course, frequently the big city, mining, or mill districts. The Republicans draw heavily in the Anglo-Saxon, Northern and Western European, Protestant districts which characterize the rural areas of the state. These ethnic and religious alignments often strongly color the politics of the district. They may in part account for, or possibly reflect, the kind of bitter, yet issueless, politics that prevail in so many quarters of the state.[35]

So it is that Pennsylvania, long a truant from the social-economic, urban-rural divisions in our national politics, has capitulated to national party patterns. Probably in the long run no state's political system can long isolate itself from the national political life. So pervasive are presidential and Congressional politics that they inevitably color and define the politics of the states. The state's Democrats have become largely the party of urban and metropolitan Pennsylvania, drawing their greatest support from the primary industrial and mining areas of the state. The Republicans, aside from footholds in high-income and some traditional urban districts, cling largely to suburban, mixed small-town and rural, and purely rural districts. The districts which are the cities over 100,000 elected almost half (fifty-three of 108) of the Democratic contingent in the 1959 legislature, while the districts in which a majority of the population lives in rural areas elected over half (fifty-four of 102) of the Republican legislators. The loyalties of the mixed urban-rural districts in between remain sharply divided.

•

This, then, is the constituency structure within which this study of party and representation takes place. These are the basic social and economic coalitions supporting the two parties and defining the dimensions and intensity of the two-party competition throughout the state.

While urban groups bemoan their underrepresentation in state legislatures across the country, Pennsylvania has by and large played by the rules of equal representation in its lower chamber. To be sure, rural, farm, low-income, white citizens have been overrepresented. To some extent, also, the House constituencies

35. Since these data are based on interview and observation rather than on census data, they are limited to the seventy-eight districts of the interview sample.

overrepresent those areas in which the Republican Party wins elections. Yet, a close approach to equal representation prevails, and few states start the race for legislative control with as few inequalities as does Pennsylvania. No party or social or economic interest is seriously or permanently handicapped in its quest for power in the House of Representatives.

For the chapters which follow, the most important conclusion of this material is the nature of the division of the constituencies between the two parties. The fact that the Democrats dominate the urban areas while the Republicans maintain a rural base influences the style of politics they practice, the social character-istics of the candidates they recruit, and the kinds of responsibility they impose on their legislators. Urban-rural differences in Penn-sylvania translate not only into differences in party loyalties, but also into differences in the "political cultures" which set local ex-pectations about what the parties should do and what or who the candidates should be.

3 • The Parties

Will Rogers once observed that he belonged to no "organized" political party; he was a Democrat. Republican wits, though not so indelibly recorded, must at times have reflected in the same vein. Disorder marks the structure of both major American parties. In style of organization alone they range from the traditional machine to the informal local party clique so common in much of rural America. Even astute scholarly attempts to classify political parties by formal characteristics seem hard put to accommodate the American parties in their schema.[1] Disorganized or not, however, the parties have a capacity for organized activity, for playing a role and exerting "muscle" in the political process.

If the contesting of elections is the chief function of the American parties, it makes sense to classify them by their ability

1. E.g., Maurice Duverger, *Political Parties* (New York: John Wiley & Sons, 1954). Duverger gives a three-part structural classification of parties based on organizational nature, membership, and leadership type.

to win those elections. We have, therefore, separated majority from minority parties, and, on the basis of their strength in inter-party competition, we have developed elegant distinctions within the ranges of one-party and two-party systems.[2] And, if the parties are simply electoral organizations, it is only a short step to the conclusion that the only relevant measure of the party's effectiveness and strength is its ability to win elections.[3] The ability to win elections has become virtually the only measure of party functioning.

But victory as the sole measure of party operation in the election processes—and hence of party effectiveness and strength —has three conspicuous shortcomings. In the first place, contesting elections involves more than drawing voters at the polls. If the party is anything more than a momentary electoral coalition, it involves itself in a series of recruitment and selection activities prior to the election. Especially in one-party districts, the meaningful steps in picking officeholders—those attempts to persuade, discourage, and support candidates before and during the primary—all precede the election. The party that surrenders control of the selection process may have to give its label and support to candidates who have no debt to it and who may even be anathema to it. More than that, it will lose its chance to reward its faithful members with a spot on the ticket. Nor can it guarantee loyalty to its party pledges and platforms. To the extent that the party shares the prenomination and nomination processes with ambitious candidates, personal cliques, interest groups, or community elites, it also shares the electing function with them.

2. Typical of recent studies which have attempted to erect typologies based on electoral percentages are Austin Ranney and Willmore Kendall, "The American Party Systems," *American Political Science Review*, XLVIII (1954), No. 2, 477–485; Joseph A. Schlesinger, "A Two-Dimensional Scheme for Classifying the States According to Degree of Inter-party Competition," *ibid.*, XLIX (1955), No. 4, 1120–1128; and Robert T. Golembiewski, "A Taxonomic Approach to State Political Party Strength," *Western Political Quarterly*, XI (1958), No. 3, 494–513.

3. Party "strength" has come to mean, consequently, success in attracting voter majorities to the party's candidates for office. The last chapter so identified the two parties in Pennsylvania.

Second, the evaluation of party as a winner or loser ignores it as a political organization. Although the American parties may not be precise in structure or tidy in hierarchy, they do have organizational characteristics which can be observed. The nature and articulation of this organization involve a potential for action on which the party draws as it plays its roles in the political system, but that organization bears no one-to-one relationship to its ability to win elections. One can hardly assume that behind every winning party stands the support of a vigorous party organization. In a number of constituencies the victorious party may do little more than lend its prestige to personable candidates.

Third, the criterion of victory is at best a partial test of the party's total electoral function. What of the Republican organization in a working-class district in central Philadelphia or Pittsburgh? One can count it unlikely that the Republicans will win many elections there in the near future. But the local minority party may perform other valuable services, despite its local losses, merely by contesting elections with full vigor, by offering attractive leadership alternatives, by mobilizing votes for candidates for state-wide or national office, and by maintaining party morale and willingness to fight again in the district. Conversely, a party may win elections in a safe district against only token opposition and play a very minor role in the enlisting of party voters for the ticket. No party can be properly evaluated and its role in the community fully understood merely by pointing to the fact that it wins or loses elections.

The problem of this chapter, then, is twofold. First, the electing function of the party must be elaborated. Apart from its successes or failures on Election Day, we need to know more of its participation in the earlier selection processes. Second, we must examine party organization and structure. Both scholars and party "pros" have long assumed that a party's ability to carry elections is in some way related to the vitality of its organization, that the well-manned and articulated party organization maximizes party chances for victory. In exploring the relation of the ability to win elections to the type of organization the party maintains, then, this chapter will examine the "salvation-through-hard-work" prescription so common in the conventional wisdom of American politics.

This orientation of political scientists to the party as elector seems to result in great part from methodological considerations. To study the party as victor, we have at hand the necessary data, officially recorded and generally available. Moreover, those imposing columns of vote totals bear the hallmarks of unimpeachable objectivity and certainty. Data on other party activities and functions must, by contrast, be ferreted out by laborious field research. They must be measured and evaluated on scales and categories of the scholar's devising. Regardless of degree of influence, it seems undeniable that, in the study of parties, the availability of data has determined both research priorities and the shaping of concepts to best accommodate the handy data.

Local Party Organization

In a formal sense, all local party organizations share characteristics imposed on them by state statute. Table 4, however, reports the distribution through Pennsylvania of four differing types of local party organization. This typology reflects the range of party organizational types presently found in the state. It is based on the degree of articulation within the organization, on the regularity of its activity, and on its internal discipline and control. Type "A" may best be thought of as the old-style "machine";

TABLE 4

DISTRIBUTION OF TYPES OF PARTY ORGANIZATION
BETWEEN THE TWO PARTIES

Type of party organization	Total (N = 156)	Democratic (N = 78)	Republican (N = 78)
	Percentage		
A	17.9	30.8	5.1
B	23.1	20.5	25.6
C	35.3	29.5	41.0
D	23.7	19.2	28.2

TABLE 5

RELATION BETWEEN VOTE FOR DEMOCRATIC CANDIDATE
AND ORGANIZATION OF PARTIES

Vote for 1958 Democratic legis- lative candidate	Democratic organizations		Republican organizations	
	A and B (N = 40)	C and D (N = 38)	A and B (N = 24)	C and D (N = 54)
Percentage	Percentage			
Less than 40	0	31.6	16.7	14.8
40–49.9	17.5	42.1	33.3	27.8
50–59.9	30.0	23.7	25.0	27.8
60 and over	52.5	2.6	25.0	29.6

consistent, almost full-time committee work, determined internal discipline, and centralization of authority mark its hierarchy. On the other hand, the "C" organizations, in which only some of the local functionaries are active, are "electoral" organizations which center their activity around the election races and in which internal discipline is sufficiently relaxed to tolerate even dissident committeemen. Type "B" organizations stand between the two; they lack the centralization of authority, the patronage incentives, and the almost professional activity of the old-time machine, and yet their organization is fuller and more active than the strictly electoral organization. As for "D," it might be called the "minimum" organization. It is in most cases a paper organization in which a handful of activists keep alive a substantially disorganized and demoralized party.[4]

There exists a close relation within the Democratic Party between these organizational types and their ability to win elections. As the party's percentage of the vote for legislator rises, so does the likelihood of a developed, alert, and unified party organization (Table 5).[5] A similar relationship exists between the type of party

4. See Appendix "B" for a complete explanation of the categories used in Table 4.
5. In fact, if one used as a complete criterion of party victory the Democratic percentage of the 1958 gubernatorial vote (instead of the 1958 legislative vote), the relation between victory and type of organization would be even more striking. Perhaps the gubernatorial vote is a better indication of the residual, long-run loyalties than is the legislative vote.

organization and the population density of the district (Table 6). That these relationships should be more dramatic within the Democratic than the Republican organizations suggests the nature

TABLE 6

RELATION BETWEEN POPULATION DENSITY AND ORGANIZATION OF PARTIES

Population per square mile	Democratic organizations		Republican organizations	
	A and B (N = 40)	C and D (N = 38)	A and B (N = 24)	C and D (N = 54)
	Percentage			
0–99	0	50.0	0	35.2
100–199	12.5	21.0	12.5	18.5
200–999	10.0	13.2	16.7	9.3
1,000–9,999	27.5	7.9	33.3	11.1
10,000–19,999	20.0	5.3	16.7	11.1
20,000 and over	27.5	0	16.7	13.0
No information	2.5	2.6	4.2	1.9

of the determinants of party organization. Two important factors associated with the type of organization—the probability of party victory and the political milieu of the densely populated urban centers [6]—work at cross-purposes for the Republicans. If a vigorous type of organization breeds in the urban, populated areas,

6. The reader will note that population density (Table 6) turns out to be a sensitive and successful correlate of party organization type. Throughout this study, that index will repeatedly prove useful. As an index, it of course incorporates the differences between urban and rural areas, but it distinguishes as well within urban and rural areas. For instance, it discriminates between the sparsely settled forested areas of one rural county and the unincorporated mining towns of another. It will distinguish between closely packed slum areas and the spaciously populated suburban development. In fact, it summarizes in one easy figure what we think of as the primary attribute of an urban place: people living in close proximity. To this extent, it actually serves the scholar as well as do all the subtle urban-rural categories. Logic also supports its validity for political research. The varieties of political activity that describe the strong party become possible and practicable where populations concentrate in small areas. It makes communication, discipline, and face-to-face contacts within the organization more likely.

then it grows in areas where Republican vote strength lags badly. The Republican seats of victory lie in the rural areas where "C" and "D" organization prevails. The attempt to separate these two factors in Table 7 indicates that, in all vote groups (the low Democratic percentages, of course, being the high Republican ones), the party organizations in the more densely populated districts have developed more fully than those in the less popu-

---

TABLE 7

RELATION BETWEEN VOTE FOR DEMOCRATIC LEGISLATOR (DIVIDED BY POPULATION DENSITY OF DISTRICT) AND TYPE OF PARTY ORGANIZATION

Vote for Democratic legislator	Population Density *	Democratic organizations		Republican organizations	
		A and B	C and D	A and B	C and D
Percentage		Percentage			
Less than 40	Low	0	10	2	8
	High	0	2	2	0
40–49.9	Low	2	14	3	13
	High	5	2	5	2
50–59.9	Low	3	7	1	9
	High	9	1	4	6
60 and over	Low	4	1	1	4
	High	16	0	5	11
No information		1	1	1	1
		40	38	24	54

* Low-density districts are those with fewer than 1,000 people per square mile.

---

lous ones. The nature of the constituency, then, appears more influential than prospects for party victory in determining type of organization.

Within the Democratic Party, the districts of party victory are those very urban districts disposed to well-articulated party organization. In these areas, and especially in the cities of Phila-

delphia and Pittsburgh, reside the disciplined, "big-stakes" organizations of the Democratic Party. The politics of hardship
which feed on jobs and favors for the unskilled and unemployed
both build and reflect the ruthlessly disciplined party machines
the Democrats have founded there.[7] Not even the tightly run
Democratic and Republican organizations out-state, effective as
they are, quite match the organizational fiber of the big-city Democratic machines. They have at their disposal not only the state
patronage, but local jobs as well. Here, active committeemen are
the rule rather than the exception; in other parts of the state, the
really active committeeman is as rare as he is valuable.

Electoral majorities taken by themselves fail to predict the
occurrence of party organization, especially within the Republican Party. The vigorous organization one associates with a unified, active party machine depends, apparently, more on the nature of the constituency than on the ability of the party to poll
majorities. The political mores and expectations of the constituency—its political "culture"—seem to have the major impact on
organization. In the urban, heavily populated regions of the state,
the community cultural patterns expect and tolerate different
party types than they do in rural areas. The political tactics that
Philadelphia, for example, might accept as a matter of course
would outrage the political sensitivities of many out-staters.

Actually, to speak of the political parties in the 154 legislative districts of the state is something of an inaccuracy. In almost
none of the legislative districts do there exist special district party
organizations. In only four of the 156 party organizations we sur-
veyed (two each in seventy-eight districts) did there exist a separate legislative district organization; even in these few cases this
special organization served chiefly for internal communication.
The county party still made the crucial decisions. For Pennsylvania, the county party remains the unit of legislative political
organization. For forty-two Democratic and forty-seven Republican parties in the interview sample, it was the prevailing party

7. For an illuminating study of Philadelphia politics with great emphasis
on the city's Democratic machine, see James Reichley, *The Art of Government,* "Reform and Organization Politics in Philadelphia" (New York:
Fund for the Republic, 1959).

organization. Where the county has more than one legislative district, the county chairman and organization usually maintain authority over all of them.

In Philadelphia and Allegheny counties, however, the local ward and borough chairmen have been granted considerable local autonomy, subject to some vaguely defined clearance by the county committees.[8] Especially in Philadelphia, the ward chairmen exercise appreciable freedom in the recruitment and support of legislative candidates. Clearance from headquarters tends to be perfunctory. This measure of independence the local chieftains regard as a traditional prerogative. County party personages in Pittsburgh and Allegheny County probably exert greater influence. There, one might say that central party officials actively share the local decisions with the local chairmen. When a legislative district includes more than one ward in the metropolitan centers, the two or more ward chairmen preside in uneasy condominium over the affairs of the district. Practical compromises —by which, for instance, one ward gets a city councilman and the other a state legislator—ease the competition inevitable in such an arrangement.

To this pattern of the domination of legislative politics in out-state Pennsylvania by the counties and in the two metropolitan centers by ward and county organizations, one major exception occurs. In eighteen districts of the sample—districts composed of less than a county and dominated by large cities or boroughs—local organizations have been granted at least partial autonomy in running legislative campaigns. Located chiefly in the densely populated counties outside of Philadelphia and Pittsburgh, these districts almost always house party organizations of the "A" or "B" style. Their independence testifies to their importance as urban or suburban centers within the county.

Where county politics dominate legislative politics, so do the county chairmen. The holders of party office wield the actual power within the party structures. Informal, *sub rosa* leadership is not the usual case. Politics in Pennsylvania are open and unabashed, and so are its political leaders. The only major intru-

8. Philadelphia is both a city and a county; the offices of the two have been consolidated.

sion into the power of the party hierarchies comes from office-holders, most frequently from county courthouse officials. Especially in the rural quarters of the state, they may share party power with the formal party leadership. The obscure figure of the county judge as silent political mover remains a common one in the Pennsylvania counties. On the other hand, the power of the party hierarchy itself is more substantial in the larger cities. Here the constituencies do not grow out of and follow established communities; they do not have, therefore, the competition of the indigenous community elites for control of the party. In any event, one rarely discovers in Pennsylvania those informal party leaders who hold neither party nor public office.

These are only general impressions from several months of interviewing in the legislative constituencies of the state. They may be naïve. One's inability to see either the hidden *éminence grise* or the all-powerful "organization behind the organization" may only betray the limits of his perception or the craftiness of his informants. Popular myth—and that myth is widely affirmed in party circles, too—has it that the Pennsylvania Manufacturers Association and the Pennsylvania Railroad exercise inordinate power in the councils of the Republican Party. Organized labor is said to play a similar role within the Democratic Party. Such powerful influences may well exist in the state-wide organization of the parties, but they are not readily apparent in the affairs of the local parties. The "devil theory of politics," popular both in and out of party circles, overestimates their presence and power. It also oversimplifies the process by which such group pressures are transmitted to the parties. It is not so much that any group runs the local party, but that the values of the group infiltrate and reflect the dominant community values, and as a matter of course they are reflected by party leadership. Although the guild of professional politicians resents the efforts of nonpolitical groups to assume the usual political functions, they cannot help but reflect and accommodate themselves to the outlook of important community elites.

The Parties as Nominators

Earlier in this chapter I suggested that the party's ability to win elections, though a valuable measure of its strength, left unsaid some important things about the party's full range of activities in the entire selection-election process. Contesting elections is a function which every party must of necessity undertake; not so with the nominating function. The direct primary, in fact, tries to discourage it. In assessing party operations, the extent of party attempts to recruit candidates and discipline its voters in the primary adds a discriminating test to that of victory.

If the party abdicates control of the recruitment and nomination of candidates, private groups and nonparty elites will take up the task. Trade unions, prominent businessmen, or even the directors of the local Rotary or country club will make the crucial decisions on who will stand for office. Or the chore of recruitment may fall to the ambitious themselves. A free-wheeling nomination politics of personality and personal followings result. In Pennsylvania, however, the parties themselves control the nominating function, often fighting off nonparty groups which would influence it. Operating in a hardy political climate, they may without fear of voter reprisal engage in recruitment practices and interventions in the primary that would raise cries of outrage in many other states.

Party attempts to control the nomination process range all the way from inveigling unwilling citizens into filling a minority party's ticket to arbitrating the many claims and bids for the nod in a majority party primary. This process may, however, be broken into halves: the preprimary recruitment of candidates for the primary and the attempts to control the primary itself. Since the first step, the preprimary recruitment, is to a large measure determined by the party's plan of action for the primary itself, we turn first to party activity in the primary election.

In discussing the role of the party in the primary, a few words in explanation of the three categories of party action may be helpful. The "open primary" in Pennsylvania, contrary to its formal meaning elsewhere, refers to one in which neither the party organization nor its leadership tries to influence the primary choice. At the very most, the party officers, especially the committeemen, act individually to support primary candidates. When the party takes "covert" action, it acts in concert, although covertly, to influence the primary. At a minimum, the party's top

53

leadership works quietly as a group to nominate an agreed-upon slate or candidate. The term "closed primary" has, again contrary to the usual scholarly usage, acquired a special definition in Pennsylvania politics. It describes the primary in which the party

TABLE 8

RELATION BETWEEN TYPE OF PARTY ORGANIZATION
AND ACTION IN PRIMARY

Organiza-tional type	Democratic action			Republican action		
	Open (N = 21)	Covert (N = 11)	Closed (N = 46)	Open (N = 19)	Covert (N = 17)	Closed (N = 42)
	Percentage					
A and B	0	36.3	78.3	5.3	17.6	47.6
C and D	100.0	63.7	21.7	94.7	82.4	52.4

takes overt, publicized action to support a candidate or candidates.

Not at all surprisingly, the "A" and "B" style party organizations intervene most frequently in the primaries of their districts (Table 8). Indeed, only one of sixty-four parties earlier characterized as an "A" or "B" type fails to make some attempt to control its primary, and all but eight maintain the "closed" primary. These few data perhaps indicate in themselves how a potent party system differs from that in states where gentler politics prevail.[9]

These moves to control the primary election occur, as do the "A" and "B" parties, in the densely populated urban areas. For instance, 71.4 per cent of the Democratic and 47.4 per cent of the

9. In Wisconsin, for instance, Republican county and ward units do not usually endorse primary candidates, and party constitution forbids the Democrats' doing so. See Epstein, *Politics in Wisconsin, op. cit.*, Chapter 5. Recently reported case studies also indicate that party role in the selection process in Oregon is considerably less important than in Pennsylvania; see Lester G. Seligman, "Political Recruitment and Party Structure: A Case Study," *American Political Science Review*, LV (1961), No. 1, 77–86.

Republican open primaries occurred in districts with population densities of less than 100 per square mile. However, none of the Democratic closed primaries and only 2.4 per cent of the Republican took place in these least densely populated constituencies. The ethos that encourages or tolerates disciplined organization apparently accepts those tactics necessary to maintain that power. The endorsement of candidates in a primary fight also becomes politically easier in heterogeneous, urban areas. Here, politics can be ruthless because they can be aloof and impersonal. In the tightly knit rural and small-town communities, personal friendships and local ties soften the party resolve. Therefore, the ability of the parties to control the primary—or at least to attempt that control—appears to be a function of both the political culture of the constituency and of the nature of party organization. That the closed primary within the Republican Party occurs almost as frequently as does the Democrats' in the urban areas and thus in the regions of Democratic strength suggests that prospects for victory have little effect on the party's role in the primary.

As logical preludes to these roles in the primaries, the parties work out related preprimary recruitment policies. Most (86.6 per cent) of the parties which run a closed primary have preceded that activity with intense, systematic recruitment of candidates (Table 9). The tie between preprimary and primary activities binds both ways. Having made a preliminary choice and encouraged a candidate to enter the race, the party can hardly leave him on his own in a pitched primary battle. A loss in the primary would embitter the importuned candidate, and it would expose the party's unwillingness to protect its recruitees. Nor can a closed-primary organization not recruit. If it did not, it would too often face a Hobson's choice in the primary and even support candidates for whom it had positive distaste. To a considerable extent, the party must either control the entire nomination process or not bother at all. To influence one part and not the other only invites the betrayal of its candidates and, consequently, its own political embarrassment. This systematic recruiting of candidates and orderly building of preprimary party tickets in Pennsylvania, though, contrasts sharply with Epstein's finding that in Wisconsin only 10 per cent of the party officials polled would admit to

TABLE 9

RELATION BETWEEN PARTY'S ACTION IN THE PRIMARY AND ITS PREPRIMARY RECRUITMENT *

Primary action	Democratic recruitment			Republican recruitment		
	Systematic (N = 48)	Moderate (N = 16)	Sporadic (N = 14)	Systematic (N = 28)	Moderate (N = 35)	Sporadic (N = 15)
	Percentage					
Open	2.1	43.8	92.9	0	28.6	60.0
Covert	10.4	37.5	0	14.3	28.6	20.0
Closed	87.5	18.8	7.1	85.7	42.9	20.0

* For explanation of the three categories of recruitment, see Appendix "B."

"even as much attempted control as is implied by trying to dissuade individuals [from running for office]." [10]

Since the preprimary and primary activities are so closely related, the type of organization which tries one tries the other. Of the sixty-four organizations of both parties identified earlier as "A" or "B" types, fifty-four engage in systematic recruitment of candidates. Although the recruiting parties can be found in all population densities throughout the state, the nonrecruiters are almost exclusively concentrated in low-density areas. Naturally, then, these fervid activities also typify the politics of the metropolitan areas; of the fifty-six organizations in the twenty-eight districts drawn from cities over 100,000, forty-one (73.2 per cent) are systematic recruiters. Only seventeen of the sixty-four party organizations operating in the rural districts (26.6 per cent) recruit as intensively.

Since we find the thorough and systematic recruiting organizations in the types of districts the Democrats usually carry, there is strong correlation between them and the electoral success of the Democratic Party. Yet, the activities of the parties before and in the primary election—their concerted attempts to control the nomination process—reflect constituency characteristics to an

10. *Op. cit.*, p. 93.

even greater extent than do the types of organization. Constituency expectations about what the parties "ought" to do, more than organization itself or likelihood of victory, mark the limits of party control of the recruitment and nominating of candidates for office.

The process by which this recruitment goes on does not lend itself to easy generalization. Primary responsibility for recruiting and ticket-building rests generally with the party chairman, although he may share it with informal leaders, party insiders, or party executive committees. In only ten of these 156 constituency parties did the recruitment power rest with special party caucuses or selection committees. Nor did nonparty groups participate with any frequency. In only eleven Democratic organizations were nonparty groups actively participating in the recruitment; nine of these were labor groups. In only seven Republican parties, six of which involved business organizations, were there similar incursions. The parties in Pennsylvania not only fend off intruding nonparty groups, but they also avoid democratic intraparty recruiting processes.

In the hard-core minority parties, recruitment often involves little more than harried efforts by the chairman and a few henchmen to fill the party ticket. At most it involves the chairman's sitting as a passive arbiter over political ambition, either blessing or vetoing the aspirations of those who for private motive want to make the futile run for office. But the powerful, active party organizations present an impressive picture as they sort out the petitions of their many willing candidates. Their main goal, of course, is to find the candidate with the best potential for victory, although that may be a lesser consideration for the solidly entrenched urban machine aware of its ability to elect virtually any candidate it chooses. Especially in these latter cases, the selection of the candidate becomes a ritual in which the party pays homage to the myth of political opportunity and propitiates and compromises the powerful intraparty followings various aspirants have.

Screening activities in these majority parties begin well in advance of the primary filing date. Although the party leadership

57

may initiate its own recruitment and screening chores, party committeemen and other worthies carry to the leadership the cases
for their favored candidates. Self-starting candidates also seek
sponsorship among the influential in the party. Nonparty groups,
such as civic organizations or unions, may petition the leadership
on behalf of their candidates. Most of the names proposed in this
initial sifting stage, of course, receive a laborious scrutiny—for
political history and party *bona fides,* for general background
and character, and for the whole spectrum of political assets from
ethnic ties to credit rating.

Eventually the party insiders, usually an executive committee, meet to fashion a slate which reflects a balanced appeal
to all the interests and localities in the constituency. Formal
courtesy may dictate that the slate be submitted to the full party
committee for ratification, but such committee action rarely involves more than *pro forma* approval. Finally, the party an-
nounces the agreed-upon ticket, still in advance of filing time, in
the hope of forestalling competing candidacies. As the primary
campaign unfolds, the party, if it pursues the closed primary, will
distribute marked sample ballots among its voters, take advertising space in the local newspapers, and through local committee
work circulate "the word" to the party adherents. Often the party
endorsement also carries with it tangible financial earnests of
support.

The Political Culture

Patterns of party organization and function do not develop
willy-nilly. The ability to win elections can encourage party organization and its influence in the nomination process. Where
the party is long deprived of the fruits of victory, it easily adopts
the defeatist and minimalist psychology of the chronic minority
party. But organizational type and, to a greater extent, party
functioning in the pre-election processes appear to be related
above all to the population density of the constituency. The significance of the factor of population density is, however, not
readily apparent. How and why should it play such an important role in the shaping of party organization and function?

First, the physical nature of the constituency clearly has its

58

impact on the parties. In the urban areas, populations are concentrated and accessible to intense party activity. In the sparsely settled rural areas, there is little opportunity for the face-to-face contacts on which the intensely organized parties build a web of personal contact, loyalty, and obligation. Furthermore, the compact urban constituency follows no natural community lines. The party there may organize and discipline its followers without competition from general community elites or resistance from close personal ties.

But, more important, the political ethos of the people of the urban areas accepts party organization and activity more readily than does that of the rural dwellers. The world of maximum and aggressive party organization reflects the more general social needs and ways of life of the urbanite. That such a political culture prevails in Philadelphia and Pittsburgh should surprise no one. But it prevails as well in many of the smaller cities and in the heavily populated, though unincorporated, coal-mining sections and steel-mill centers of the state. In these areas, the parties have traditionally been social workers and father confessors, finding jobs for the unemployed, shielding the unfortunate from economic insecurities, and playing intermediary with the austere organs of government and justice. Where the authority of the local committeeman has been a protective one, local residents have come to associate party organization and activity with desirable consequences for themselves. The party in the urban centers has, furthermore, provided political cues and leadership for the unassimilated, ignorant urban minorities and given meaning to the confusion of politics and government.

The development of this ethos, this expectation, occurs quite independently of party preference or auspices. When the Republicans counted the votes of the urban constituencies in their electoral coalitions, they, too, established powerful political machines there. Even today the Republican organizations in these areas bear many signs of fully developed party operation. When in the city, the parties meet the cities' political expectations.[11]

11. Where the Republicans continue to control the smaller cities, such as Harrisburg and Wilkes-Barre, they maintain strong political organizations there.

The issue of political mores and expectations has another crucial dimension. The urban political culture so favorable to partisan organization reflects at the same time the ethnic-racial cleavages in the state. The ethnic groups of Northern and Northwestern Europe predominate in those constituencies with the less well-developed party organization of "C" and "D" types. Ethnic minorities, so often the victims of social and economic prejudice, are, on the contrary, associated with the more fully developed organizations. One may wonder whether they have found in the party not only a protector, but also a ladder to higher social and economic status. Reichley suggests so in his comments on party leadership in Philadelphia:

> . . . for the Irish, Jewish, Italian bright boys who pursue it, politics is a "status-conferring" occupation. The Bill Greens and the Victor Blancs and the Aus Meehans, they point out, could no doubt have earned wealth and even the respect of their fellowmen by selling insurance, practicing law, and the like. But the one thing that they could not earn in these ways is "place" in the community. Politics gives them that. As successful politicians, they can demand deference from the greatest capitalists, the toughest union leaders, the oldest of the old families. The Protestants, on the other hand, the argument continues, have "place" conferred upon them as their natural birthrights, and many may rise in society through the practice of the more normal professions; it is for this reason that so few Protestants are to be found in the dirty trade of politics.[12]

The egalitarianism of the political machine and its power in the community have traditionally offered these groups a promising means of breaking out of their social cul-de-sac. Finally, these minorities may hold fewer of those antipolitical attitudes and values with which the American middle class perceives the political party so warily.

Whereas the nature of political organization itself may be greatly shaped by electoral strength, the limits of its growth and its role in the nomination process seem largely dependent on these local political mores. It is the constituency rather than the party which sets the outer limits, the boundaries of acceptability, for

12. *Op. cit.*, pp. 104 f.

both the party organization and its functions. Even in areas in the big cities where they are hopelessly overmatched at the moment, the Republican Party organizations still openly endorse primary candidates. Perhaps the thesis of a political culture is merely that political parties, like any other political or social institution, have only a limited autonomy, that they must respond to and serve the needs and expectations of the social groups for which they function.

Summary
When the party loses, the folklore of politics blames the loss on poor and ineffective organization. The well-oiled political machine, however elusive it may be in reality, remains the ideal and the goal of the experienced politician. These data suggest, however, that a third factor—the variations in political culture associated with urban-rural differences—complicates what would seem in the lore to be a simple relationship. Full-time, effective, and even aggressive organization results in part from the constituency's political expectations. Party victory at the polls will not necessarily produce it, nor will it necessarily produce victory. Those elements of party strength which we associate with aggressive political organization have, in other words, their main roots outside the two-party struggle.

Party function, exemplified here by party activities in the nomination process, depends even more than organizational characteristics on political culture. Political culture, understandably, has its greatest impact on the party's overt activities, that aspect of party of which the constituency is most likely to be aware. Its internal organization remains at least one step removed from local awareness. Organizational structure develops both in response to its anticipated or tolerated functions and to the rewards the party can expect in its election contesting. Expediency and common sense dictate that a party structure on the nature of a Pittsburgh ward committee will scarcely be needed to execute the minimal functions of a losing rural party.

In short, the development of party organization and operation can in part be explained in this fashion:

1. The political ethos or culture of the constituency plus its

physical characteristics (such as density of population and arrangement of communities and subcenters) limit what party organization and operations can be. Their impact is greater in shaping party function, such as that in the nomination process, than in influencing party organization.

2. Within these limits, the party's potential for carrying elections also shapes the type of party organization. Majority and minority parties within the same constituency often develop differently in response to the differing roles and incentives the vote division allocates to them.

3. Only secondarily does the type of party organization itself determine what the party will do and how it will do it. It does that because, like any organization, it constitutes a potential for activity.

4. The resultant syndromes of organizational types and activities produce a series of "political styles"—distinctive political ways of life—within the varied constituencies of the state.

•

Even though the American parties are indeed great, stable conspiracies for the capture of public office, to judge them solely in terms of electoral success exaggerates one portion of the total recruitment and nomination function. The election itself is only the culmination of what may have been a long train of activity which the more aggressive parties have begun months or years before—when, perhaps, two disconsolate committeemen discussed candidates likely to turn present defeat into victory two or four years later. Even more dangerous is the easy assumption so common in the conventional wisdom of American politics that certain organizational types and patterns of activity accompany the winning party because, as wisdom's logic would have it, they are essential ingredients of that victory. A generation of careful and intensive studies of the electoral bases and successes of the American parties has told us far more of the party voters and their motivations than of the parties themselves. If these scanty data have at least raised some questions about what we do not know of party organization and activity and about their relation to the two-party struggle, they will have served their purpose.

4 • The Candidates

Perhaps no aspect of the legislative process has been
so thoroughly studied as the personal characteristics of the legislators themselves. Knowledge of their ages, occupations, and recent political histories is not difficult to come by, and it lends a
flesh-and-blood realism to the austere data of legislative roll calls.
The many studies of the lawyer as the dominant occupational
group in American legislatures typify this general approach to the
legislative process.[1] Since the legislator's values, goals, commitments, predispositions—call them what one will—reflect his social experience, we attempt to surmise his values and loyalties
from that experience. Thus we study the social characteristics

1. Joseph A. Schlesinger, "Lawyers and American Politics: A Clarified
View," *Midwest Journal of Political Science,* I (1957), No. 1, 26–39, and David
Derge, "The Lawyer as Decision-Maker in the American State Legislature,"
Journal of Politics, XXI (1959), No. 3, 408–433, are recent examples.

of the American legislator for clues to his legislative behavior.[2]

Perhaps, however, the value of these social-background studies might better be seen another way. Both the party and the constituency as broad systems of political loyalties try to select legislators who reflect those socially acquired values and loyalties. In other words, the party selects men with years of experience in the party hierarchy, men presumably, therefore, attuned to the values and interests of the party. The recruiting elites of the constituency exert their influence to select candidates who will, if elected, respond to constituency values rather than to those of the party. In this concern with the values of candidates for office, we look for influences which the candidate has internalized through his experiences and group affiliations.

The last chapter indicated clearly that the Pennsylvania parties intervene freely and positively in the election and pre-election processes. These data on the candidates themselves should, then, tell something of the criteria the parties have in mind as they go about the recruitment chore. What do they look for in a candidate that will at the same time ensure his political appeal to the electorate of the constituency and his loyalty to the party? What do the characteristics of Republican and Democratic candidates tell us of the recruitment processes within the two parties and of the popular images the parties bear? Social-characteristic studies indicate not only the roots of legislative behavior but suggest as well the nature and objectives of the political recruiters.

Studies of this type inevitably raise a third issue—the problem of representation in a democracy. This issue lies beyond the scope of this study, but brief mention may be made of it. Data about public officials always reveal that they are not in any way a cross-section of the American electorate. They invariably raise the question whether a representative not himself typical of his

2. The whole spate of studies of the social characteristics of state legislators, largely culled from state government manuals, must rest on the assumption that there is some relation between the representative's social experience and his actions as a representative. For a broader approach to the problem of the social characteristics of official decision-makers, see Donald Matthews, *Social Backgrounds of Decision-Makers* (Garden City, N.Y.: Doubleday, 1954).

constituents can fully represent their political goals and aspirations. Can or should the constituency pressures which conflict with internal pressures ever prevail? Something of the issue is caught up in the two meanings of the verb "represent." It suggests a principal-agent relationship, and yet at the same time it means "to symbolize" or "typify." Although this chapter will not resolve this normative question of democratic procedures, it will offer some data about the ways in which the Pennsylvania legislators typify their electorates and the ways in which they do not.

The subjects of this chapter are the 106 legislators and the 106 men and women they defeated in 1958 in the seventy-eight legislative districts of the interview sample. Of the 106 legislators, we interviewed 105; one was ill and absent for almost all the session. Since two of the elections were uncontested (the Republicans offering no opposition in Greene County or the Second District of Erie), there were in reality only 104 defeated candidates, and ninety-five of these were interviewed. Eight of the nine not interviewed were Republicans, and, of the nine, six would not consent to an interview or seemed to evade one; the other three escaped our searches.[3] Of the six defeated Republican candidates who refused an interview, all were political novices who were recruited by the party to run hopeless races in urban areas. They averaged 37.5 per cent of the popular vote in their districts, and none polled more than 42.4 per cent of the vote. Most had, apparently, been stunned by the campaign and election and had reacted with bitterness and disenchantment to the whole business of politics.

Social Characteristics

The accessibility of data on their age, education, occupation, and public offices in the meager biographies of legislators printed

3. The missing nine came from these districts: Allegheny Twelve and Fourteen; Bucks One (the single Democrat); Luzerne Three; Philadelphia Three (two candidates), Nineteen, and Twenty-eight; and Washington One. All of the other data were obtained in the personal interviews described in Appendix "A." None came from legislative manuals or directories, and only one interview was supplemented by a mailed questionnaire. However, in our other interviewing it was possible to obtain some information about the nine defeated candidates and one legislator who were not interviewed.

TABLE 10

SEX, RACE, AND AGE CHARACTERISTICS OF 1958
LEGISLATIVE CANDIDATES

		Legislators		Defeated candidates	
	Totals	Demo-crat	Repub-lican	Demo-crat	Repub-lican
Characteristics	(N = 212)	(N = 54)	(N = 52)	(N = 52)	(N = 54)
		Percentage			
I. Sex					
Male	94.8	92.6	94.2	94.2	98.1
Female	5.2	7.4	5.8	5.8	1.9
No information	0	0	0	0	0
II. Race					
White	95.8	94.4	100.0	98.1	90.7
Negro	2.8	5.6	0	0	5.6
No information	1.4	0	0	1.9	3.7
III. Age					
20–29	1.9	0	0	3.8	3.7
30–39	17.0	16.7	17.3	21.2	13.0
40–49	25.9	29.6	17.3	34.6	22.2
50–59	33.0	33.3	38.5	28.8	31.5
60–69	12.3	14.8	17.3	5.8	11.1
70 and over	2.4	1.9	5.8	1.9	0
No information	7.5	3.7	3.8	3.8	18.5

in state manuals and yearbooks has already stimulated consider-able study.[4] Consequently, one begins a "profile" of American

4. The number of these studies is virtually beyond counting, and, in addition, numerous studies of broader scope include this kind of analysis; representative and useful studies include Charles S. Hyneman, "Tenure and Turnover of the Indiana General Assembly," *American Political Science Review,* XXXII (1938), Nos. 1 and 2, 51–67, 311–331; William T. R. Fox, "Legislative Personnel in Pennsylvania," *Annals of the American Academy of Political and Social Science,* CXCV (1938), 32–39; Charles S. Hyneman, "Who Makes Our Laws?" *Political Science Quarterly,* LV (1940), No. 4, 556–581; Paul Beckett and Celeste Sunderland, "Washington State's Lawmakers: Some Personnel Factors in the Washington Legislature," *Western Political Quarterly,* X (1957), No. 1, 180–202.

state legislators with some expectations about what he will find. For instance, in Pennsylvania males dominate the legislature, just as they dominate all American political life (Table 10). Pennsylvania Democrats appear slightly more tolerant of lady politicians than do the Republicans, but in neither party are they widely recruited for the legislative race. In many sectors of the state, social understanding of the female role hardly admits of women voting, much less of their seeking public office. The popular image of the representative is at least implicitly male. Legislative chambers in the states often bear the signs (for example, finely burnished cuspidors) of the male club, and a woman legislator may be viewed as an intruder into smoking-room company.

All but 3 per cent of the 1958 candidates in the sample were white. That 3 per cent compares with a 6.1 per-cent non-white figure in the 1950 census (and 7.6 per-cent by 1960) for the state as a whole. What assures some Negro representation in the House is their concentration in the city of Philadelphia; all but one of the six Negro candidates were from Philadelphia.

A recent updating of Hyneman's pioneering study of state legislators found that some 71 per cent of the legislators in lower houses fell within the age bracket thirty through fifty-nine.[5] In the present study, a similar 76 per cent of all the candidates were within that range (Table 10). Epstein's recent work sets the median age for Wisconsin legislators at forty-nine,[6] close to the median of fifty years for the 1958 Pennsylvania legislative candidates. In view of the aging of the American population in the past generation, though, it is surprising to find that the Pennsylvania legislators of 1958 were actually younger than they were twenty-five years earlier. Studies of two sessions in the mid 1930's found median ages of fifty-one and fifty-two for the state's legislators.[7] Pennsylvania, too, finds younger men on the Democratic ticket than the Republican (forty-eight to fifty-two years) and younger men among the losers (forty-eight to fifty-two years).

Although no substantial differences in age, sex, and racial

5. Beckett and Sunderland, *op. cit.*, p. 193.
6. *Op. cit.*, p. 106.
7. Fox, *op. cit.*, p. 34.

characteristics between the two parties emerge, differences do appear in educational and religious data (Table 11). Only three of the twenty-four legislators who did not graduate from high school were Republicans, and more Republicans than Democrats attended college. Most surprising is the small decline in Pennsylvania since the 1930's in the percentage of legislators who attended college or university. In 1935, some 54 per cent of them had some college training,[8] but in 1958 only 48 per cent of the candidates and 51 per cent of the legislators had spent any time in collegiate halls. The state legislators, of course, compare favorably here with the entire population of the state; in 1950, only 31.2 per cent of those Pennsylvanians over twenty-five years had even finished four years of high school.

Although differences in educational level of Democratic and Republican legislators are marked, the differences between the losers of the two parties are not. In fact, the defeated Democratic candidates are actually a better educated group than the defeated Republicans. This inversion of party differences between the legislators and the defeated candidates will recur repeatedly in the tabulations of these social characteristics. Clearly, the differences between the legislators of the two parties are not party differences; they do not grow out of the party's expressed preference for specific social types. They are differences imposed by the constituencies. The unsuccessful candidate tends to resemble the successful candidate (and, therefore, the district's image of the legislator) more than the victorious candidates of his own party running from other constituencies. The local constituencies stamp their marks on the candidates by defining political acceptability and availability. Candidates conform to constituency expectations rather than to any party image formed by its legislative winners.

Among the legislators, the Democrats prevail among the Catholic, Jewish, and Orthodox memberships, and the Republicans can be found overwhelmingly among the Protestants. Again, among the defeated candidates, little difference appears (Table 11). The Democrats clearly do not enter the lists with Catholic

8. *Ibid.*, p. 37.

TABLE 11

EDUCATIONAL AND RELIGIOUS CHARACTERISTICS OF 1958 LEGISLATIVE CANDIDATES

Characteristics	Totals (N = 212)	Legislators Dem. (N = 54)	Legislators Rep. (N = 52)	Defeated candidates Dem. (N = 52)	Defeated candidates Rep. (N = 54)
			Percentage		
I. Education					
8 or fewer years	7.5	18.5	1.9	7.7	1.9
9–11 years	11.3	20.4	3.8	3.8	16.7
High school graduate	31.1	24.1	28.8	34.6	37.0
Attended college	13.7	13.0	17.3	15.4	9.3
College graduate	10.4	3.7	19.2	13.5	5.6
Advanced degree *	21.2	20.4	28.8	23.1	13.0
No information	4.7	0	0	1.9	16.7
II. Religion					
Roman Catholic	33.5	57.4	7.7	34.6	33.3
Lutheran	14.2	7.4	25.0	9.6	14.8
Presbyterian	12.3	5.6	23.1	9.6	11.1
Methodist	10.8	5.6	19.2	13.5	5.6
Episcopalian	3.8	5.6	5.8	0	3.7
Baptist	2.4	3.7	0	0	5.6
Miscellaneous Protestant	3.8	0	7.7	3.8	3.7
United Church of Christ †	5.2	1.9	5.8	9.6	3.7
Jewish	5.7	9.3	0	9.6	3.7
Orthodox	1.9	3.7	0	1.9	1.9
Quaker	1.4	0	3.8	1.9	0
No affiliation	0.9	0	1.9	1.9	0
No information	4.2	0	0	3.8	13.0

* Thirty-eight of these forty-five advanced degrees are LL.B's.
† Ten of these eleven members of the United Church of Christ were members of the Evangelical and Reformed Church.

candidates in the Republican "Bible Belt" counties of the state. Nor do the Republicans run Lutherans or Presbyterians in the Italian and Irish wards of Philadelphia. The thirty-five Catholics of the 106 legislators in the sample account for 33 per cent of the group. The National Council of Churches estimates that Roman Catholics constitute 46.4 per cent of the church membership (*not* total population) in Pennsylvania.[9] Of the legislators, 5 per cent are Jews, compared with the 5.7 per-cent figure of the NCC. Obviously, then, the Catholic population of the state is under-represented and the Protestants overrepresented in the Pennsylvania House. The various Protestant denominations share legislative representation in close to the same proportion as among the churchgoers of the state as a whole. Lutherans have 27.9 per cent of the legislative Protestant membership and 26.9 per cent of the state's Protestants, the Presbyterians 24.6 and 17.2, the Methodists 21.3 and 18.6, the Episcopalians 9.8 and 6.9, United Church of Christ 6.6 and 8.0, Evangelical United Brethren 1.6 and 6.5, and Baptists 3.3 and 3.8. To some extent, these major and prestigious Protestant bodies are overrepresented at the expense, not only of the Catholics, but also of the smaller, less socially acceptable Protestant churches. The Church of the Brethren and the Disciples of Christ, which total 3.2 per cent of the state's religious membership, count no legislators among their members.

Turning to the candidates' occupations classified by census categories, the Republican legislators hold higher-status occupations, the Democrats the lower ones (Table 12). The main difference between the two parties' legislators lies in the fact that all fourteen of the legislators who work at blue collar jobs are Democrats. Surprisingly, the Republicans, often thought of as the party of the white collar worker, have fewer legislators in the clerical and sales occupations than the Democrats. Of the thirty-six legislators in the professional and semiprofessional categories, twenty are attorneys (eight Democrats and twelve Republicans).[10]

9. *Churches and Church Membership in the United States* (National Council of the Churches of Christ, Series C, No. 9, 1957).

10. Three more legislators are graduates of law schools but are not now practicing law.

The category of "proprietors, managers, and officials" includes twenty-six (fourteen Democrats and twelve Republicans) legislators (of thirty-seven) who are owners and managers of small businesses—clothing store, ice-cream factory, car dealership, jewelry store, or real-estate brokership, for instance. Six of the remain-

TABLE 12

OCCUPATIONAL CHARACTERISTICS OF 1958
LEGISLATIVE CANDIDATES

Occupational category	Total (N = 212)	Legislators		Defeated candidates	
		Dem. (N = 54)	Rep. (N = 52)	Dem. (N = 52)	Rep. (N = 54)
		P e r c e n t a g e			
Professional, semi-professional	27.8	25.9	42.3	30.8	13.0
Farmers, farm managers	5.2	5.6	7.7	5.8	1.9
Proprietors, managers, officials	36.8	31.5	38.5	28.8	48.1
Clerical	6.1	3.7	1.9	9.6	9.3
Sales	5.7	7.4	5.8	3.8	5.6
Craftsmen, foremen	7.5	14.8	0	13.5	1.9
Operatives	5.2	9.3	0	3.8	7.4
Service (including domestics)	1.4	0	0	0	5.6
Laborers (including farm)	.9	1.9	0	1.9	0
No information	3.3	0	3.8	1.9	7.4

ing (five of them Republicans) are management executives. The other major occupational categories are smaller and fairly self-explanatory.[11]

11. A fuller explanation of and index to these categories can be found in the Bureau of the Census' two explanatory volumes issued with the 1950 census reports: *Alphabetical Index of Occupations and Industries* and *Classified Index of Occupations and Industries*.

Since only twenty of the 106 legislators are lawyers, they sit in fewer numbers in Pennsylvania than in many other states. Whereas one-third of the Wisconsin legislature recently practiced law,[12] this sample has only 19.2 per cent. In Pennsylvania twenty-five years ago, 36 and 42 per cent of the House membership were lawyers in two different sessions.[13] And recent counts in Illinois and Massachusetts find between 26 and 31 per cent lawyers.[14] Interestingly, Pennsylvania's 13.5 per cent workers in the legislature, though probably higher than in most states, remains markedly below the 26.1 per cent sitting in the state House in the 1935 session, following the great Roosevelt sweeps of the early 1930's.[15]

One should, however, warn against facile comparisons. Given the differing economies of the two states, a comparison of the percentages of farmers sitting in the Pennsylvania and Kansas lower houses would foolishly ignore differences between the two states. The same comparison, or one within a single state over time, may also deceive in failing to consider the partisan composition of the legislatures. Of greater usefulness are the comparisons with the occupational composition of the state as a whole, and, in this regard, the Pennsylvania House of Representatives is hardly representative of the state's working force. The 59.9 per cent of the state's labor force who are "working men and women," for instance, are matched by only 13.1 per cent of the sample legislators.[16] Conversely, although professional and proprietarial groups make up only 16.1 per cent of the state's working force, they account for 68.9 per cent of the legislators in the interview sample. The defeated candidates generally represented an occupational distribution similar to that of the legislators, except that party differences are by no means as sharp and in some cases are reversed.

12. Epstein, *op. cit.*, pp. 105f.

13. Fox, *op. cit.*, p. 35.

14. Gilbert Y. Steiner and Samuel K. Gove, *Legislative Politics in Illinois* (Urbana: University of Illinois Press, 1960), p. 3; Duncan MacRae, "The Role of the State Legislator in Massachusetts," *American Sociological Review*, XIX (1954), No. 2, 186.

15. Hyneman, "Who Makes Our Laws?" *op. cit.*, p. 574. Hyneman's definition, however, includes salesmen and clerks.

16. "Working men and women" are here defined to include craftsmen and foremen, operatives, service workers, and laborers.

These occupational data fairly scream that the state legislator's job is a part-time one and that legislators must come from
occupational groups with flexible work responsibilities. The lawyer may be able to crowd his gainful labors into the legislative
schedule, but the clerk or office manager cannot. They indicate,
too, that the lawyer in Pennsylvania, as elsewhere, is vocationally
the community's politician. He possesses the verbal skills we
associate with the legislative life, and his very training in the
law singularly equips him, in the eyes of most voters, to make
law. Furthermore, these overrepresented occupations are the ones
which create public contacts on which to build a political career.
The lawyer, auctioneer, insurance salesman, farm-implement
dealer, to mention but a few, establish in their business or profession the wide circle of acquaintances so necessary for political
success. One of the defeated candidates in the sample had established his quota of personal contacts and friendships by operating
carnival rides through the summer at volunteer firemen's carnivals
in his district.

These occupations, by the same token, are the ones which
will profit from the contacts the legislator makes or from the
"ethical advertising" an active candidacy yields. It is almost the
classic career pattern for the new young lawyer in town to build
his practice in part through the pursuit of public office. Finally,
as perhaps the best single indicator of social status, the occupations of the candidates indicate the measure of status and success
we expect of our representatives. Not necessarily the most prestigious occupations, they are eminently respectable, often affording
upward mobility. To sum up, the legislator's occupation must
offer a number of assets: free time, public contacts, favorable
vocational training, and social status. The occupation of the
lawyer in American society offers them all par excellence.

These occupational patterns also betray some information
about the Pennsylvania political system. The party differences in
occupation point to the alignment of working groups with the
Democrats, but party differences are not otherwise so great as in
other states.[17] Perhaps economic class lines, as they are reflected

17. Key, *American State Politics, op. cit.,* pp. 259 f., for instance, says
that "most" businessmen in the Michigan legislature are Republicans.

in occupational loyalties, are not so sharply drawn as they are elsewhere. Second, the fact that in Pennsylvania the underrepresentation of wage employees is not so drastic may point to the moderating effect of strong party organization in the recruitment and selection process. When the party in reality picks the candidates, it may soften the pressures of the local status system and select men more typical of the party's voters.

Legislative candidates in Pennsylvania have especially deep roots in the state. All but eight were born in the United States, and 171 of the 199 on whom we obtained information claim Pennsylvania as their native state. Furthermore, 74.1 per cent of the Democratic winners and 73.1 per cent of the Republicans were born in the very county from which they were elected. Of the defeated candidates, 51.9 per cent of the Democrats and half of the Republicans were born in the counties they sought to represent. And, though 11 per cent of the 1950 population over twenty-one had been born abroad, only 3.8 per cent of the candidates were. In a further reflection of this localism, all but four of the legislators (two of whom live in newly developed suburban areas) have resided for thirty years or more in their present home county. These facts raise the pull of localism to something of an iron law in Pennsylvania. In fact, 68.9 per cent (seventy-three of 106) of all the legislators had lived all their lives in their present county of residence. The losers of 1958, though less exclusively products of their home constituencies, counted fifty of their number (47.2 per cent) as lifelong sons of the present county of residence. Only 19.2 per cent of the Democratic losers and 3.7 per cent of the Republican had lived in their present county for less than twenty years.

The local ties, moreover, extend beyond the present generation. The fathers of more than one-half (113) of the 1958 candidates were born in the state, and eighty-four of them were born in the same county in which their son or daughter was in 1958 seeking election to the state legislature. In the birthplaces of the fathers, one again begins to see differences between the two parties. Of the thirty-two legislators with fathers born abroad, twenty-four were Democrats—exactly two-thirds. They reflect the Democratic

74

appeal to first- and second-generation ethnic groups, particularly
of Ireland and Southern and Eastern Europe. Again there prevails
the "mirror effect" among fathers of the losing candidates; the
fathers of the Republicans rather than of the Democrats tend
to be foreign-born. The Republicans running in the powerfully
Democratic ethnic enclaves of the Pennsylvania cities have simply
adopted the ethnic coloring of the constituencies.

Doubtless this overpowering drive to recruit the long-time
sons of the area reflects the absence of recent population influxes
and migrations within Pennsylvania. One would hardly expect to
find the same phenomenon in Florida, California, Arizona, or
Nevada. Yet its existence indicates a pervasive localism in the
politics of Pennsylvania. The mantle of office, apparently, falls
on the life-long resident of a family well-established in the county.
For all practical purposes, this unwritten native-son rule excludes
great numbers of potential candidates. Shut off from public office
are those highly mobile young "organization men" who are
reputed to move from one city to another across the nation as
they move up the corporate ladder. Excluded, too, are the lawyers
and other young professionals who go to a new county to build
a career. Excluded, really, are all but the old families of most
counties. This localism, however, runs deep in American politics
and is certainly not restricted to Pennsylvania. Key has described
one of its manifestations, the "friends and neighbors" appeal,
in the politics of the American South,[18] and Epstein reports also
that over 70 per cent of the Wisconsin legislators a few years ago
had lived in their home counties over thirty years.[19]

Social Status

Taken together, the information on the social backgrounds
of the 1958 candidates indicates that legislators and legislative
candidates come from the "second-rung" elites in the status system

18. Key, *Southern Politics in State and Nation* (New York: A.A. Knopf,
1950).
19. *Op. cit.,* pp. 105 f. This percentage is still well below Pennsylvania's
91.5 for the same data, even counting the five legislators on whom we have
no information.

75

of the district. They are of established, reputable, good-name families; they are engaged chiefly in the professions and small business; and they are enrolled in the service of Rotary, public charity, and one of the large local churches. Rarely are "The 400," the distinguished old families, the envied wealth, or even the pillars of the country club represented. Although the sons and grandsons of these favored families have been increasingly involved in the presidential and gubernatorial politics of the states, they rarely take an active and public role in local or state legislative politics. Politics at the local level remain the province of the middle or upper-middle status groups, who may find in it an avenue upward in the local status system. Holding the legislative seat provides new access to influential circles and offers the legislator contacts and opportunities that may raise his economic status as well as his social prestige.

To explore the relationship between social status and political recruitment more systematically, we attempted—fully aware of the perils—to rank the social status of the candidates in each constituency.[20] Rather than attempting to place the candidates in any defined "upper-middle" or "lower-upper" classes, this was merely an attempt to place the candidates wherever possible in rank order of social status. Four factors, weighted evenly, guided the rankings—occupation, group membership, residential area, and ascription of status by local community leaders.[21] Where

20. The reader will note that this attempt to rank social status does not take into account *economic* status. We decided early that questions about the candidates' annual incomes would be futile; the resulting information would often be questionable, and the question would antagonize some respondents. For a critique of the methods of ranking and judging social status and a catalogue of the problems in each, see Milton Gordon, *Social Class in American Sociology* (Durham: Duke University Press, 1958). In the ranking we have done here of the candidates from each district, one special problem deserves note. Where the constituency is large, the candidates may live in separate parts of it and not come within the same status system. Obviously, ranking becomes impossible in such cases.

21. In ranking the factors by social status, the following guides were used: Occupation—Cecil C. North and Paul K. Hatt, "Jobs and Occupations: A Popular Evaluation," *Opinion News* (September 1, 1947), 3–13, and the Bureau of Census categories which range in attributed status from professionals through laborers. Group membership—the status values here vary from community to community, but exclusive city clubs generally stand at

TABLE 13

SOCIAL STATUS RANKING OF 1958
LEGISLATIVE CANDIDATES *

	Legislators		Defeated candidates	
Rank of social status	Dem.	Rep.	Dem.	Rep.
I. *One-member districts*				
First	13	17	3	14
Second	14	3	17	13 †
Cannot rank	6	4	4	6
II. *Two-member districts*				
First	3	8	0	2
Second	3	7	0	3
Third	3	0	8	2
Fourth	2	0	7	4
Cannot rank	4	1	1	4

* Candidates from the three- and four-member districts have been omitted because their small numbers make analysis difficult.

† In order to make the tabulation symmetrical (that is, to record the same number of defeated Republicans as victorious Democrats), we have arbitrarily assigned a status rank of 2 to the Republicans for each of the two elections in single-member districts which they did not contest.

differences did not seem clear-cut or where the candidates lived in two entirely different social orbits, we made no attempt at an arbitrary ranking. Not unexpectedly, the Republicans as a group showed markedly higher social status than did the Democrats (Table 13). Even the defeated Republicans maintained an equality of status with the Democrats who beat them.

the top, followed by country clubs, tennis clubs, the top service clubs (such as Rotary), other service organizations, business and professional groups, fraternal organizations, (in which an important subhierarchy exists), ethnic and national organizations, and labor organizations. Residential area—the greatest status generally attaches to residence in exclusive residential suburbs, followed by recent suburban developments, older upper-middle class neighborhoods, mass-produced developments, older single-dwelling areas, multiple-dwelling urban areas, older multiple-housing areas near industrial areas, and deteriorating and slum areas. Obviously, this residential ranking bears a close relationship to market value of the units in an area.

TABLE 14

OCCUPATIONS OF FATHERS OF 1958 LEGISLATIVE CANDIDATES

	Legislators		Defeated candidates	
Occupational category	Democrat (N = 54)	Republican (N = 52)	Democrat (N = 52)	Republican (N = 54)
	Percentage			
Professional, semi-professional	5.6	19.2	3.8	5.6
Farmers, farm managers	7.4	25.0	15.4	5.6
Proprietors, managers, officials	29.6	29.6	28.8	22.2
Clerical	5.6	1.9	0	0
Sales	1.9	0	5.8	5.6
Craftsmen, foremen	25.9	9.6	15.4	13.0
Operatives	11.1	3.8	21.2	9.3
Service (including domestics)	1.9	3.8	5.8	3.7
Laborers (including farm)	11.1	3.8	1.9	13.0
No information	0	1.9	1.9	22.2

If one accepts occupation as an index of status, then the father's occupation may be taken as a mark of the social prestige the candidate's family enjoyed in the community. These data (Table 14) for the 1958 legislative candidates reinforce the previous rankings of status. The occupations of the Democratic legislators' fathers differ sufficiently from those of the Republicans to indicate difference in the status background of the candidates' families. That the candidates as a whole pursue more prestigious occupations than their fathers (compare Table 14 with Table 12) testifies to their upward social mobility and ambition.[22]

22. Again, this reliance on the census categories accepts their premise of a rough approximation of status ranking to the order of listing the occupational categories.

The implication of this social status disadvantage for the Democrats should be pointed out. Voters in most constituencies favor candidates with higher status, with the aura of success and acceptability about them. The Republican Party, increasingly the party of the *arriviste*, the comfortably wealthy, the successful, has a corner on the socially prestiged community leadership. Even were the Democrats inclined to match country club member with country club member, they would be sorely pressed to find them. What reservoir of candidates both able and acceptable to the community are the Democrats to tap? [23] In many parts of the country, union leadership has been the answer for the Democrats, but many Democratic county organizations in Pennsylvania have refused to accept union-sponsored candidates for fear of being too closely associated with organized labor. Even when the local Democratic organization succeeds in finding a member of the community elite who may have traditional ties to the Democratic Party and is willing to run for office, it often accepts a candidate who is ideologically indistinguishable from the Republicans. The need to present high-status candidates, then, works against program or issue distinction between the parties.

Finally, a word about the organizational affiliations of the 1958 legislative candidates seems in order. They are with few exceptions "joiners" par excellence. Whether out of real gregariousness or a feeling that it is politic, they collect memberships instead of stamps, coins, or matchbooks. Even though concrete information is difficult to evaluate—largely because "membership" can signify so many degrees of loyalty and involvement—their organizational affiliations tend to fall into patterns. The Mason-service club syndrome and a Moose-Elks-fire company pattern tend to typify the Republicans. Memberships in the Knights of Columbus, Odd Fellows, and ethnic groups (such as the Sons of Italy), not to mention labor unions, occur more frequently among Democrats. Among the service clubs, still as influential in small-town America as when Sinclair Lewis wrote, twenty-eight

23. Key, *American State Politics, op. cit.,* pp. 256 f., makes the same point.

legislators report active memberships in Rotary, Lions, or Kiwanis; six of them are Democrats and twenty-two are Republicans. Among the losers, eight Democrats and nine Republicans belong to one of the three. Organizational differences between the two parties are greatest among the legislators; 20.4 per cent of the Democratic winners in the sample had no active nonparty affiliations, whereas only 7.7 per cent of the Republican winners had none. At the worst, such an emphasis on organizational ties may produce the "professional toastmaster" or community huckster, the man who "influences" people as an indoor sport. But at best it yields men and women genuinely committed to the community's welfare and supporting that commitment with work in the Little Leagues, in United Fund drives, or on the hospital board. It would not be amiss to call these joiners the "go-getters" of the community. Even though academics and intellectuals may dismiss them as Babbitts, they fill the average community's picture of the local leader.

In seeking candidates, party organizations, especially in the nonmetropolitan districts, prize these organizational affiliations highly. Participation in a wide range of public activity ensures that the candidate has at least a modest circle of acquaintances, that he is gregarious and a "good mixer," that his peers have found him socially acceptable, and that he will be known for his interest in the community. Parties particularly cherish affiliations that have about them the aura of decency and wholesomeness. Nothing succeeds better than religion and sports. The list of 1958 candidates abounds in candidates known in their districts for Sunday solos with the church choir, lay-preaching throughout the district, ardent temperance sentiment, or superintendence of a local Sunday school. As for sports, large numbers of the candidates had won high school athletic fame, coached local sports, held active membership in sportsmen's clubs, or belonged to a local "boosters' club." Of the three male candidates in the First District of Lehigh County, for instance, one sponsored softball teams, another was the public-address announcer at the local football games, and the third originated an annual banquet honoring local high school athletes.

80

Finally, both parties and constituencies insist on a more rudimentary form of social acceptability. The candidates must be "respectable" in whatever ways local mores define that term. Socially, it means that they must not engage in behavior the community finds precious or affected, activities thought effete, highbrow, or pretentious. Morally, its implications are even more elusive. In some quarters of the state, such criteria are not inordinately demanding, but, especially in rural areas, prevailing morality may frown on the divorced man, the social drinker, and the general "high liver." As one county chairman explained, "In this county you just can't win an election with gambling, guzzling, or golf."

Paradoxically, voters seem to want both the typical and the atypical in their elected representatives. In certain characteristics —religion, race, ethnic background—they compel the parties to select candidates in their own images. Yet they favor candidates with education, occupation, and general social status far above the average. They seek the successful, the respected man—the common man writ large, so to speak. What they get, given both their demands and the opportunities of political life, are often ambitious, upward-mobile representatives of the background and parentage typical of large numbers of voters in the district. Inevitably, their criteria for the legislative candidate work to the advantage of the Republican Party, which finds it easier, because of its electoral base and group support, to produce candidates who meet these community specifications.

Political Background

Just as legislators acquire values and interests from social experience, political experience invests them with political values, mores, and skills. If political parties and partisan organization mean anything in the legislative process, the legislator with political experience and party ties ought to respond differently than those with none. Furthermore, to place the 1958 quest for a legislative seat in the context of wider political experience helps us to discover its place in political career patterns. Just as we can determine what advantage the seat in the legislature has for the socially anxious, we can discover what political gains it has for the politically ambitious.

In terms of previous legislative experience, the differences between winners and losers in 1958 are as great as one would suspect. Whereas only thirteen (12.3 per cent) of the defeated candidates had ever held a seat in the House, only nineteen (17.9 per cent) of the winners were first-termers who had *not* held one. Among the incumbents, more Democrats than Republicans had had no experience, but the median length of service in each of the parties was two sessions' experience. The percentage of newcomers (17.9) in the sample of legislators stands considerably lower than the 26.0 and 32.6 figures for the state in 1935 and 1937, respectively, and far below the over 50 per-cent turnover in the lower house of the Washington legislature from 1941 to 1951. It is, though, similar to the 15 per-cent figure recorded recently in Illinois.[24] At the other extreme, thirty-two of the 106 legislators (30.2 per cent) in this Pennsylvania sample had won election to the House for five or more earlier sessions, as against the 22.0 and 16.3 percentages for the state in 1935 and 1937.[25] And 35.8 per cent had attended more than three previous sessions, about 6 per cent more than in Wisconsin in recent years.[26]

Clearly, the Pennsylvania legislature tends to greater experience and longer tenure than the lower houses of other states. The longer tenure of the Pennsylvania legislators suggests that the seat in the House does not figure importantly in the career patterns of the politically ambitious. Obviously, they do not move on to greener political pastures as quickly as their counterparts

24. Fox, *op. cit.*, pp. 36 f. Doubtless this figure reflects the great political change and turnover of the 1930's, especially within the suddenly victorious Democratic Party. See also Beckett and Sunderland, *op. cit.*, pp. 181 f. The Illinois data is from Steiner and Gove, *op. cit.*, p. 4. The difference between these and the present Pennsylvania figures may result from Steiner and Gove's discounting those "new" legislators who had earlier legislative experience.

25. Fox, *op. cit.*, p. 37.

26. Epstein, *op. cit.*, p. 103. Again, it is important to note that the Epstein data for Wisconsin include both the state Senate and Assembly and for that reason are not completely comparable.

in other states. As later data will show more clearly, election to the House tends to come at the end of a political career or constitute something of a career in itself. Moreover, the strength of the parties in recruiting and electing legislators, and especially in controlling the primaries, cuts down legislative turnover. Not so long ago, a tradition of "two terms and out" prevailed in many of the rural Pennsylvania counties, and any legislator who defied its Jacksonian injunction incurred considerable voter displeasure. That tradition is presently dying, largely at the parties' insistence, a victim of growing awareness in county party organizations of the values to them of legislative seniority in Harrisburg.

If there exists any defined political career pattern in Pennsylvania, election to the House does not appear to be a part of it. Only one legislator, a Republican, had held as many as three other public offices, and only eight (seven of them Republicans) had held two others. As of 1958, seventy-one of the 106 legislators in the sample had been elected to one or no other public office, and sixty-seven of the 106 (63.2 per cent) had held no other elective position than their legislative seat; sixty-three of the defeated candidates had never held public office of any sort (Table 15).[27] With such a paucity of previous officeholding, talk of these candidates' "political careers" would be pretentious. Only the office of school director appears with any frequency in the political histories of the candidates, and these almost exclusively in the nonmetropolitan areas. However, for that minority of the candidates with some officeholding experience, one may generalize that it is exclusively at the local level. Little of it (only six cases, to be exact) involves even county office. If there is an order of accessibility to public office, the state legislature in Pennsylvania apparently stands just above small-city, borough, and township office, below county and large-city office, and greatly inferior to state-wide or national office. Certainly within Philadelphia and

27. Seven legislators and seven defeated candidates, in addition to these, have been appointed to offices that would normally be elective. In most of these instances, they were appointed to fill the term of an officeholder who had died in office.

TABLE 15

NUMBER AND TYPE OF OFFICES PREVIOUSLY HELD
BY 1958 LEGISLATIVE CANDIDATES

Public office (including House), held prior to 1958	Legislators		Defeated candidates	
	Dem.	Rep.	Dem.	Rep.
	Percentage			
I. *Number held*	*(N = 54)*	*(N = 52)*	*(N = 52)*	*(N = 54)*
None	20.4	7.7	55.8	63.0
One	53.7	51.9	32.7	14.8
Two	24.1	25.0	9.6	5.6
Three	1.9	13.5	0	3.7
Four	0	1.9	0	1.9
No information	0	0	1.9	11.1
II. *Office held*				
School director	8	9	7	6
Minor judiciary *	2	6	4	2
Burgess	0	2	0	0
Township supervisor	2	4	0	2
Borough councilman	1	5	6	0
Miscellaneous †	2	4	9	3
	15	30	26	13

* Includes justice of the peace, alderman, and magistrate.
† Includes tax collector, mayor, borough auditor, township auditor, constable, city councilman, assessor, county commissioner, district attorney, sheriff, county auditor, and city controller.

Allegheny counties, election to the House ranks as only a medium-sized political plum, less desirable than local elective office or many local patronage jobs.

By venturing after few other offices, the 1958 candidates at least spared themselves the bruises of defeat. Only thirty-six of the legislators had ever lost a run for public office, and, of these, twenty-six lost earlier races for the House. Only ten of the legislators had ever been defeated seeking another office, but thirty-one of the defeated candidates had, a fact which suggests that minority parties tend to rely on the same men to carry the flag

84

repeatedly in losing causes. So, not only had the 1958 candidates not held offices other than the legislative seat, but they had not waged many losing candidacies either. The quest for a House seat is apparently not the midpoint or conclusion of carefully developed or nurtured political careers. The age of the average candidate plus the long tenure of the elected suggest that it will not be the beginning in many cases. Election to the House very likely serves either as a middle-grade reward for long party service or as a modest plum and opportunity for public service for community leaders of limited political aspirations.

But political experience and involvement may extend even beyond the career of the candidate himself. He may come from a family immersed in politics, and, if he does, he gains a double advantage. He receives a formidable political education and at the same time acquires a political name. Scholars have generally found that politics runs in families, that men seeking public office often come from families active in political life.[28] Pennsylvania is no exception. A total of thirty-four (fifteen Democrats and nineteen Republicans) of the 106 legislators (30.4 per cent) reported their fathers active in politics, either as a candidate for public office or as a holder of party office. The defeated candidates followed a pattern of less activity; fourteen Democrats and seven Republicans reported active fathers.

By several tests, the legislators and defeated candidates of this sample had toiled long and faithfully in the party ranks. The fact that seventy-nine of the 212 candidates (37.3 per cent) had held patronage jobs in Pennsylvania, under federal, state, or local auspices, testifies to their political services. In fact, 13.7 per cent of all the candidates and 23.1 per cent of the losing Democrats had held two or more patronage positions. These jobs ranged over a wide spectrum—an executive position in the state service, an inspectorship in the field services, the superintendency of a county highway crew. Considering the realities of political sponsorship in Pennsylvania, one may safely assume that these ap-

28. See Eulau, Buchanan, Ferguson, and Wahlke, "The Political Socialization of American State Legislators," *Midwest Journal of Political Science*, III (1959), No. 2, 193.

pointees had either records of political activity or very good political connections. This high incidence of political job-holding may also tell us something of these candidates' motivation for political activity. Significantly, six of the defeated Democratic candidates acquired state patronage positions between November, 1958, and the summer of 1959, during which we interviewed them. Several other job-holders were doubtless pressed into candidacy as a price of keeping theirs.

Strikingly, all but sixty-four of the candidates (69.8 per cent) had held some party office before 1958 (Table 16). And forty-nine of the candidates had held one party office or another, for a cumulative total of more than ten years. Close to one half of them (93 of 212) had served as party committeemen; another sixteen had been ward or district leaders; fourteen had been party leaders in a borough, township, city, or special district party organization. At the county level, four of the candidates had been county chairmen, four had been state committeemen, and another thirty-nine had been officers of the county organization or sat on the executive board; six had been officers in the county women's organizations, and seventeen had held office in the local Young Democratic or Young Republican organization.[29] In both the number of years in party office and in the variety and types of offices held, there exists little difference between the candidates of the two parties.

Finally, the candidate's level of party activity and influence also reveals the nature of his ties to the party (Table 17). This index is largely an ascriptive one, and, although its categories are defined as accurately as possible,[30] placement of the candidates in one of them demands a difficult decision. Information

29. Some men held more than one of these two offices; the total is, therefore, greater than the number of individuals concerned. The number of thirty-nine in county party office is to some extent padded by the policy of many county organizations of putting the elected legislator on the executive board or committee *ex officio*.

30. Briefly, these categories were defined as follows: "None"—the candidate is neither active nor influential in party affairs; he does not campaign or in any other way work for the party; he holds no party office; he is not even generally identified with the party organization; he may be a "new face" or an unknown. "Minimum"—the candidate does little party work;

TABLE 16

LENGTH OF TIME IN PARTY OFFICE OF 1958
LEGISLATIVE CANDIDATES *

		Legislators		Defeated candidates	
	Total	Dem.	Rep.	Dem.	Rep.
Years	(N = 212)	(N = 54)	(N = 52)	(N = 52)	(N = 54)
			Percentage		
None	30.2	27.8	34.6	32.7	25.9
1–2	5.7	1.9	0	15.4	5.6
3–4	7.5	5.6	9.6	3.8	11.1
5–7	3.8	1.9	3.8	7.7	1.9
8–10	3.3	5.6	3.8	0	3.7
11–15	9.0	13.0	9.6	5.8	7.4
16–20	2.4	1.9	1.9	3.8	1.9
21–30	5.2	9.3	1.9	5.8	3.7
31 and over	6.6	9.3	5.8	1.9	9.3
Held office; cannot					
say how long	23.1	24.1	28.8	21.2	18.5
No information	3.3	0	0	1.9	11.1

* Years are computed consecutively even if offices were held simultaneously.

gathered in the interviews in the constituency plus ascriptions of influence and activity by party leaders guided the decision. The data reveal that party influence presently ranks higher among the incumbents than among the defeated candidates. That result, however, is to be expected. Election to the legislature usually

what he does is mostly on his own behalf and exclusively at local party levels; he holds no party office and exerts no influence in the party except as a candidate or officeholder. "Moderate"—the candidate campaigns for himself and others and carries some burden of work for the party; he usually holds a minor party office, such as a committeemanship; at most he possesses a position of second-line influence within the party, but he is not privy to inner councils and high-level decisions. "Great"—the candidate either holds high party office or is in the top decision-making elite of the party organization; his position is in the inner corps of the party leadership, and he participates in making party policy on selection of candidates, finances, and the like.

TABLE 17

PARTY ACTIVITY AND INFLUENCE OF 1958 LEGISLATIVE CANDIDATES

Index of activity and influence	Total $\overline{(N = 212)}$	Legislators		Defeated candidates	
		Dem. (N = 54)	Rep. (N = 52)	Dem. (N = 52)	Rep. (N = 54)
	Percentage				
None	9.9	11.1	7.7	13.5	7.4
Minimal	30.2	16.7	32.7	38.5	33.3
Moderate	38.7	37.0	38.5	42.3	37.0
Great	18.9	35.2	21.2	3.8	14.8
No information	2.4	0	0	1.9	7.4

brings an automatically amplified voice in local party matters. As a result, well over half the legislators (thirty-seven Democrats and thirty Republicans) exerted at least "moderate" influence in their party councils, holding some party office, working in party campaigns, or participating in some of the party decisions. These figures suggest, of course, that, in recruiting and endorsing candidates, the parties favor the loyal, trusted, and experienced party men and women. They can offer the legislative seat as a reward and at the same time ensure loyalty and reliability among their elected officeholders.

So it is that the legislative candidates bring to their work greater background and experience within the party system than in public elective office. Clearly, the parties prefer to pick and support their own party loyalists in the nomination process. A seat in the Pennsylvania House does not seem to fit into a well-defined stepladder of public offices up which the ambitious climb. Perhaps, however, in a state of strong party politics, one should not differentiate between party and public office in the individual's political career. In terms of the Pennsylvania political system, election to the House of Representatives often comes more as an extension of, and reward for, years of party activity than as the next step up a scale of elective offices.

Constituency, Party, and Candidates

The politics of most of the legislative constituencies grow out of a homogenous community. The dominant values of the community result from its social characteristics, and these values are in turn imposed on all who would rise to positions of community leadership. The candidates for public office must reflect, at least in basic social affiliations, the constituency if they are to win its confidence and support. It is this fact rather than any systematic party policy that accounts, for instance, for the relation between Catholic candidates and the Democratic Party. The outsider, the stranger to the way of life of the community, stands little chance of breaking into any political elite. No matter how long he lives in the district, the atypical remains a newcomer. So the community stamps its image on its candidates for public office by demanding that they have absorbed the majority values from a background similar to that which predominates in the district.

These basic social characteristics to which the constituency demands conformity include, first of all, race. The small number of Negro candidates in the 1958 legislative races all came from heavily Negro districts, and other predominantly Negro districts still dominated by white political leadership and candidates were threatening to end that domination. Religion is another of these basic characteristics. If one looks at the Democratic and Republican candidates from predominantly Protestant and non-Protestant constituencies,[31] the impact of the religious composition of the district becomes evident (Table 18). Even discounting party differences, the distinction is considerable; Protestant candidates, despite party, came from Protestant districts, and Catholics tended to seek election in non-Protestant districts. These religious differences parallel ethnic differences. All impressionistic evidence here points to constituencies picking candidates having the dominant ethnic and national backgrounds of the constituents. These "birth-

31. The data used here on the religious composition of the districts were obtained from constituency interviewing and observation; they were described in Chapter 3.

TABLE 18
RELIGION OF 1958 CANDIDATES RELATED TO RELIGION OF CONSTITUENCIES

Religion	Protestant Districts		Non-Protestant Districts	
	Democrat (N = 65)	Republican (N = 65)	Democrat (N = 41)	Republican (N = 41)
	Percentage			
Roman Catholic	30.8	10.8	70.7	36.6
Protestant	55.4	84.6	19.5	46.3
Jewish	9.2	1.5	9.8	2.4
No religion	1.5	1.5	0	0
No information	3.1	1.5	0	14.6

right" social characteristics—race, religion, ethnic and national background—tend, then, to be givens in the availability formulas to which candidates must conform. In addition, the constituencies demand that their candidates resemble them in the most obvious way of all—residence. The odds against the election of a newcomer of only twenty or twenty-five years' residence remain prohibitively high in Pennsylvania.

Other social characteristics, however, escape the district's pressure for conformity. In the name of success, status, and the popular conception of "qualifications" for the legislative job, they permit the atypical. In occupation, educational level, organizational affiliation—those classic determinants of social status—the candidates do not typify their districts. But do these characteristics change within broad categories of districts—within urban-rural differences, perhaps? They do not seem to. These candidate characteristics are apparently fairly evenly distributed across the constituencies of the state. Nor are these social characteristics in any way related to the nature of the parties in the district. Strong parties which actively try to control primaries, for instance, do not select candidates differing in social attributes from those of other party organizations.

It appears, then, that the constituency desire to elect high-

status candidates occurs evenly over the state. This matter of
the variation of status characteristics is, however, subject to an
important political distinction (Table 19). As a party becomes
a majority party, it acquires a social acceptability that in turn
enables it to recruit candidates of more impressive social stand-
ing. Its character as a winning party also makes its ballot more
attractive to the ambitious. As the chances for Democratic victory

TABLE 19

STATUS RANK OF 1958 CANDIDATES BY POLITICAL
COMPLEXION OF DISTRICT

| | Percentage of legislative vote won by Democrats | | | | | | | |
| | 0 = 39.9 | | 40 = 49.9 | | 50 = 59.9 | | Over 60 | |
Status rank	Dem.	Rep.	Dem.	Rep.	Dem.	Rep.	Dem.	Rep.
First	0	10	4	15	5	12	11	7
Second	8	3	9	10	12	5	7	9
Third	2	1	6	1	3	1	2	2
Fourth	3	0	6	1	1	3	2	2
Fifth through eighth	4	2	3	1	1	0	1	1
Cannot rank	1	2	5	5	5	6	5	7
Totals	18	18	33	33	27	27	28	28

in the district increase, so does the social status of the Democratic
candidates. By the time the district becomes a rather solidly Democratic one, the Democratic candidates are even slightly outranking
their Republican opponents. Of course, Republicans greatly out-
match their opponents in the safe Republican seats.

In terms of social background, the 1958 legislative candidates,
then, come by and large from the socially rising men and women
of the constituency's prevailing racial, religious, and ethnic-
national groups. They are in every way "local boys [and girls]
made good." Election to public office provides many of them
an ideal opportunity for early achievement of their personal goals.
It offers them the prestige, opportunity, and access their ambitions

91

demand. And, from the parties' viewpoint, they constitute excellent officeholding material—not wealthy or prestigious in their own right, little inclined to rebel against the status-conferring community elites, and neither financially nor socially independent. In short, they are a vulnerable social group, dependent on the help and recognition of the mighty. That they and the parties discover such a mutually satisfactory alliance testifies to the pragmatic art with which the political system builds on nonpolitical interests.

The political characteristics of the legislative candidates are also related to the constituencies. The reader will remember that types of party organization were earlier (in Chapter 3) associated with a combination of the electoral strength of the party in the constituency and the constituency's political culture. Those varying organizational types produce candidates to match their varying political styles. The highly developed party organizations selected men who were more active and influential in party affairs than did other parties. For instance, legislators from the "A" and "B" parties had held party positions for a median of thirteen years; those from others had only four years' experience. Similar figures for the two groups of defeated candidates are 10.5 and 4.5 years.

Nor can this relation between party organization and the candidates' party service be explained in terms of the likelihood of winning the election. In the winning parties, the candidates have generally longer records of party service and influence, but those of the consistently minority parties have more party ties than do those of competitive parties. In the minority parties, the hierarchy serves as fodder for the hopeless local races. Patronage-seekers often dominate these persistently minority parties; they run for office more in hope of winning patronage than public office.

Similarly, the candidates of the highly developed parties do not seem to have markedly greater public officeholding experience than those of the weaker organizations. If one counts the years of such experience among the candidates, little difference emerges between the two sets of party organizations. In fact, the more casual organizations have more candidates with officeholding records over ten years long. Since the active parties are majority ones more often than not, it is all the more surprising that candidates from these parties have no more experience in public office. Perhaps the "A" and "B" political organizations can more freely select candidates without a political pedigree or political name. Although they may no longer be able to elect any warm body upon which they decide, the highly mobilized party organs can and do elect virtual unknowns to office.

Considering the incidence of active party organizations in urban, densely populated parts of Pennsylvania, it is not surprising that the urban and rural candidates evince different political characteristics. The political path of the urban legislator often leads from party service to Harrisburg. The candidates from cities of 100,000 or more have a median of three years of office-holding experience, but the candidates from the rest of the state have five. By the same token, the candidates from the big cities as a group wield greater influence within their party organizations (Table 20). The political way of life in the metropolitan centers decrees that public office may, and even ought, to be used to reward the party's faithful. Especially in the smaller urban centers and suburban areas, the candidates and the party leadership appear to be more nearly separate.

The political differences between urban and rural legislators,

TABLE 20

RELATION BETWEEN URBAN-RURAL NATURE OF
CONSTITUENCY AND THE DEGREE OF PARTY
INFLUENCE OF CANDIDATES

Degree of party influence	Majority of population living in:		
	Cities over 100,000 (N = 70)	Other urban places (N = 58)	Rural places (N = 84)
	Percentage		
None or minimum	25.7	50.0	45.2
Moderate	44.3	41.4	32.1
Great	27.1	8.6	19.0
No information	2.9	0	3.6

growing out of differences in their political constituencies, reinforce the unflattering image many rural political leaders have
of their urban brethren. The average urban legislator in Pennsylvania is, indeed, more likely to be a creature of the party and
possess all the related attitudes of unswerving fealty to the party
than is his rural counterpart. Furthermore, he has probably had
less experience in discharging public responsibility, less chance
to acquaint himself with public issues, and less opportunity to
learn the little skills of maneuver and accommodation that make
for effectiveness in the legislative arena. The career pattern of the
average rural and small-town legislator better equips him to take
part in the legislative process. Without doubt, these variations in
political history help reinforce rural political power in the Pennsylvania legislature, and probably in those of many other states.

•

These were the candidates who sought a place in the Pennsylvania House of Representatives in November, 1958. As individuals, they were by no means typical of the adult population of
the state, and yet their atypicalness was not without pattern or
order. The constituencies apparently set a series of social criteria
for their candidates—criteria compounded of adherence both to
the dominant birthright characteristics of the district and to expectations that the candidate bear the marks of success, status,
and achievement in whatever ways the district reckoned them.

As to their political characteristics, the 1958 candidates were
clearly graduates of a vigorous party system. The parties succeeded
in recruiting men and women with considerable party and political training. And yet the constituencies and their varying political
cultures influenced the parties' ability to set political criteria
for their candidates. To a noticeable extent, the same political
expectations which shape the parties themselves and their political styles also shape the image in which their candidates must be
cast. The resulting legislators are products of the political socialization processes of both party and constituency. They are very
likely deeply committed to the values and interests of both.

5 • Recruitment and Selection

Contrary to the expectations of some partisans of a free and open primary, no political stork has ever brought candidates into the world. If the party cannot or will not take that responsibility, other organized centers of political power—personal followings, party factions, interest groups, or local community elites—will. When they do, the selection and presentation of candidates falls to groups that do not have to carry the final responsibility for the candidate in the campaign and election or for his eventual performance in office.

In the United States, the direct primary has severely modified, if not actually compromised, the party's role in nominating candidates. In the name of democratic values, party organizations and hierarchies must share the crucial nominating power with even the least committed partisans and the most casually affiliated voters. In the open-primary states, the party must even share it with those capricious voters who drift into its primary in search of electoral excitement. In losing control of nominations, the

American party has lost not only one of its chief *raisons d'être* but a powerful weapon for cohesion and discipline as well.

Concern about the effect of primaries on the parties is not limited to the fear that it takes the final nomination choice from the parties. By opening a direct route to nomination, the primary encourages self-starting, independent, and nonparty candidacies. It tends to strip the party of the entire recruitment and selection function, from the initial encouragement or discouragement of candidates down to the final selection or rejection. Consequently, the party often finds its traditions and symbols expropriated by men hostile to it, men from whom the party can claim no loyalty and on whom it cannot impose the checks of responsibility.

The parties have not, however, been defenseless before the direct primary. In some states, preprimary conventions and endorsements have successfully imposed party discipline on the primary. More frequently, the parties have discovered that primary vote turnouts are usually small and that a small, cohesive party group to which "the word" has been passed can generally nominate its own men. Or they have discovered the sanctions by which to veto or discourage errant candidacies. Although some evidence indicates that the primary tends to diminish two-party competition by concentrating the real political choice in the majority party,[1] we have little real information about how the parties, especially the strong and vital ones, have tried to tame the primary. Nor have we any clear notion of how candidates emerge or of how the party and primary affect their plans and chances for election.

Should the parties lose control of the recruitment and selection process, the loss would deprive them of a crucial function. Not only would party responsibility be impossible, but party itself would be enfeebled. What V.O. Key has written of the recruitment of state-wide candidates applies with equal force to the entire matter of candidate recruitment:

Perhaps the most important function that party leadership needs to perform is the development, grooming, and promotion of candi-

1. Key, *American State Politics, op. cit.,* Chapter 6.

dates for state-wide office. Although striking exceptions may be cited, it is in its inadequacy in this role that the most grave shortcoming of party leadership is to be found. To assert that party leadership of many states develops candidates is more an attribution of a duty stated in the textbooks than a description of real activity. . . . It may well be that the primary by depriving party organization of its most important function has contributed to the atrophy of party organization.[2]

In a broader sense, the recruitment process extends beyond the strength and determination of even the most powerful party apparatus. Two great recruiting agencies, each with its separate set of expectations, merge in the complex process of selecting candidates. One of them, the constituency, fixes the broad standards we speak of collectively as "acceptability" or "availability" —the congeries of social and political criteria demanded of those who would represent us. These constituency criteria, the result of the constituency's political culture as well as its social characteristics, were sketched in the last chapter. Within the broad outlines of constituency expectations, the special recruiting agencies, be they party or nonparty groups, set more specific criteria in controlling the mechanics of recruitment. Theirs is the task of planting the seeds of ambition, of tapping one aspirant or another, of preventing a debilitating primary fight. They improvise and choose within the limits set by the constituencies.

Something has already been said of recruiter and recruited in the two previous chapters. From the descriptions of party and candidate, one may infer a great deal about the elusive operations of this recruitment process. This chapter will describe that process more fully, as it is reflected in both the personal recruitment histories of the candidates and the more formal impact of the primary and general elections on them.

To generalize or even speculate about the nature of the political bug is, of course, a singularly risky business. The candidate gets it or catches it, but in ways and for reasons that often defy his memory or his candor. One can ask legislative candidates why they decided to run for the House, who asked or encouraged

2. *Ibid.*, p. 271.

them to run, and what role the party played in this decision. But what one often gets is a selected and codified version of the story which probably magnifies the candidate's political independence and power, carefully trims and brushes up his political goals and ambitions, and considerably devalues his debt to the party or other nominating groups. Not often will a legislator or defeated candidate admit that he sought election to the state legislature for the additional salary or to stimulate a flagging law practice—though some will. Candidates more frequently discuss their motives in the terms and symbols they know to be socially acceptable for seeking public office. Generous portions of the humility and conspicuous high-mindedness the American electorate seems to demand mark their accounts.

When one leaves motivation and gets to the mechanics of seeking office—the approaches of powerful recruiters, the contacts with party leaders, the ultimate role of the party—these are generally public matters to which a number of individuals have been witness. The reports of candidates, party leaders, and local observers in these matters did not often directly contradict one another; much more common were multiple versions of the same facts, each of which was the most flattering to its relater. Consider the case of the 1958 candidate of modest social status, mixed occupational history, and few group associations who was recruited by party leaders to make the legislative race to the surprise of many onlookers. According to the candidate, the party hierarchy had traditionally recruited from "The 400" of the county, but "couldn't elect them" and eventually turned to a "man of the people." Party leaders explain that they asked any number of better-known men to run, were turned down by all, and finally out of sheer desperation yielded to the candidate's well-known desire to run.

The Decision to Run

Why do they run? The great majority of the incumbent legislators (eighty-one) ran in 1958 because they were incumbents and wanted to retain their seats in the House. For them, legislating is a vocation; the legislative seat is its own excuse for being sought.

For these incumbents, the prime decision was made at least several years earlier, in the initial candidacy for the legislature. For the greatest number of candidates, whether their first candidacy was in 1958 or earlier, interest in and fondness for politics and public affairs appear the chief rationalizations for seeking office (Table 21).[3] As a reason, it carries a notable middle-class and non-

TABLE 21

REASONS FOR CANDIDACY

(Initial Legislative Candidacy of 1958 Candidates) *

	Legislators		Defeated candidates	
Reason for candidacy	Dem. (N = 54)	Rep. (N = 52)	Dem. (N = 52)	Rep. (N = 54)
	Percentage			
Interest in politics, public affairs	22.2	38.5	19.2	7.4
Was asked to run	24.1	25.0	23.1	16.7
Obligation for public service	7.4	9.6	3.8	3.7
Desire to help district	5.6	7.7	15.4	9.3
Promote ideology, interest	13.0	1.9	5.8	13.0
Dissatisfied with incumbent legislator or party	7.5	1.9	21.2	24.1
Miscellaneous (including personal)	16.7	9.6	5.8	5.6
No information	3.8	5.8	5.8	20.4

* See Footnote 3.

political respectability. Almost the same number of candidates professed to have run for the legislature initially because they were prevailed upon to do so, usually by the party. Such an explanation, of course, often begs the question and mistakes the

3. In this and the following tables, the information is for the candidate's first candidacy for the state House of Representatives. For most of the incumbents, that time was some years prior to 1958; for the defeated candidates, it was usually the 1958 primary.

occasion for the cause. In many instances, it was simply a Pennsylvania expression of the old tradition that the office seeks the man. Some, however, did run largely at party request or insistence, especially where prospects of victory were poor and the party was having difficulty filling the ticket. Ideological interest or involvement occupies a relatively unimportant place in the candidates' motivational systems.

Curiously absent from the reasons for candidacy are the personal ones. One does not expect the candidate to say that he ran to feed his ego (several, however, did say exactly that), even though the quest for office attracts more than its share of men and women obsessed with themselves and preoccupied with winning recognition and acceptance.[4] To be sure, a few candidates spelled out amazingly frank reasons for officeseeking: general boredom with their current occupation, need to supplement an inadequate income, or need to feel useful or keep busy after retirement. Most, however, cloaked their decisions in impersonal rationalizations, regardless of what local partisans accepted as common knowledge about their motives. In all states, undoubtedly, questions of this sort would evoke responses which mix the actual motives of candidates with their understanding of what are considered high and noble motives for seeking public office. In any event, the reasons for seeking legislative office in Pennsylvania appear to be no different from those in other states.[5]

4. I do not know how one goes about proving the Lasswellian contention that the political personality displaces private needs and goals in the public quest for power, nor am I certain that I would want to accept the full theoretical implications of Lasswell's statement of political personality. But that it does operate as a motive in selection to the Pennsylvania legislature is indisputable. See Harold Lasswell, *Power and Personality* (New York: W.W. Norton, 1948).

5. The reasons given in these two paragraphs rather closely approximate those reported for New Mexico in Charles B. Judah and Dorothy P. Goldberg, *The Recruitment of Candidates from Bernalillo County to the New Mexico House of Representatives, 1956* (Albuquerque: Department of Government, University of New Mexico, 1959). However, the open-ended questions of the present study did not elicit the "prestige" and "honor" answers of their study. See also Eulau *et al.*, "The Political Socialization of American State Legislators," *Midwest Journal of Political Science*, III (1959), No. 2, 201 ff., which finds little emphasis on the quest for power or influence and little ideological emphasis.

The winners and losers of the 1958 election, however, indicated differing reasons for seeking legislative office. Among the defeated candidates, one finds a whole set of reasons which themselves reflect the outlook of the outsider and the minority party. The candidate ran because he disapproved of the majority party or of the whole state administration, because he wanted to strike a blow for the two-party system, or simply because he wanted to beat the incumbent legislator. Furthermore, the losers, especially those from weak party organizations, were principally the ones who claimed to be running to promote the constituency's welfare and interests. In contrast to this loser's syndrome, the elected legislators adopted the nonpolitical generalizations for seeking office. More than twice as many winners as losers cited fondness for politics and the desire to perform public service. These reasons were also more common in the rural than in the urban areas of the state and, consequently, more common among Republican legislators than among the Democrats. The reflections of the victorious apparently produce a set of softened, nonpolitical, and somewhat self-congratulatory reasons for seeking office.

The partisan reasons follow no such discernible pattern. Urgings of party may be in any event only camouflage. Where it is the genuine reason, it occurs in both the strong party, where party beckons as a reward, and in the weak one, where party pleads as a necessity. What ideological reasons were cited came largely from the urban centers—and, as a result, from Democratic winners and Republican losers.

The process of encouragement, suggestion, and enticement leading to candidacy remains only somewhat less obscure than the candidates' motivations. Party minions clearly make the contacts. The candidates overwhelmingly noted that some representative of the party encouraged or asked them to run for office (Table 22). Only a shade more than 20 per cent of the incumbents reported on their first candidacy for the House, whether it was in 1958 or earlier, that their encouragement came from nonparty sources. From which level in the party hierarchy the recruiter comes depends largely on the nature of the constituency and party structure within it. In the rural areas and those parts of the state in which the county is the legislative constituency, the county

TABLE 22

SOURCES OF RECRUITMENT

(Initial Legislative Candidacy of 1958 Candidates)

	Legislators		Defeated candidates	
Recruiter	Dem. (N = 54)	Rep. (N = 52)	Dem. (N = 52)	Rep. (N = 54)
	Percentage			
Party chairman or leader	13.0	11.5	13.4	26.0
Party chairman and party elite	26.0	19.2	36.5	26.0
Local political active(s)	9.3	7.7	15.4	13.0
Nonparty group	7.4	7.7	3.8	0
Nonparty individual(s)	13.0	13.5	5.8	1.9
None *	26.0	36.5	17.3	22.3
No information	5.6	3.8	7.7	11.1

* Most of these candidates, however, eventually contacted party leader-ship or other community groups for encouragement and/or approval.

chairman and executive committee do the honors. In the heavily urban areas, the contacts tend to be local party workers. No differences appear between candidates of the two parties in the general pattern of their recruitment.

Although those candidates who were approached by no recruiters were the true self-starting ones, we made another attempt to identify the self-starters by asking the candidates whether the initial idea of running for the legislature originated with them or someone else. Over half of each party's legislators reported that the notion of running was theirs; just over 40 per cent of both the Democratic and Republican losers reported similarly. Of the winners, 20.4 per cent of the Democrats and 25 per cent of the Republicans attributed the decision to the party; among the losers, 42.3 per cent of the Democrats and 26 per cent of the Republicans ran at party request. Furthermore, about another 10 per cent of all the candidates thought that the idea of running belonged both to the party and to themselves. But nowhere are

102

the differences between candidates of the two parties significant.

The issue of the self-starting candidacy is, of course, far more complex than these data suggest. Under the flattering stimulus of party hints and overtures, the candidate-to-be may develop ambitions or may at least make the party's will his own. By the same token, he may become the object of party encouragement only after he has carefully hinted his availability or his contemplation of a candidacy. But, regardless of the tangled relationships between party and candidate, party is obviously the chief stimulus to candidacy in Pennsylvania. In only eleven instances (5.2 per cent) did the candidates report that the idea of running originated with a nonparty group or individual.

In both parties, the defeated candidates more frequently than the winners indicated that the idea of their running originated wholly or in part with the party. Furthermore, the losers were far less frequently recruited by nonparty sources than were the winners; only 1.9 per cent of the defeated candidates were so recruited. Their responses perhaps indicate the presence of drafted candidates in districts where prospects of election are dim or worse. The self-starting candidates—those who claim to have originated the idea of their own candidacy—appeared with almost equal frequency in both parties and in all categories of party strength. The strong party organizations, with their vigorous interventions in the primaries, do not discourage the self-starters. In fact, the very incidence of self-starters may force them into more vigorous attempts to regulate primary competitiveness.

The Decision to Let Them Run

Motivation, determination to run, encouragement by influential sources—these are the makings of a candidacy. But, in a state of strong party rule, the final hurdle to candidacy remains the party's formal reaction to the individual's plans. The legislative candidates generally encountered little opposition from their parties in 1958 (Table 23). They were either unopposed in the primary or supported, actively or covertly, by the party. Only four faced party opposition, and another six ran against the opposition of a few party leaders or a part of the party leadership.

103

Only ten candidates, less than 5 per cent, ran against and beat even fragmentary party opposition in the primary. Many of the candidates who had no party opposition received the formal support of the party. In some of these cases, the endorsement was

TABLE 23

PARTY SUPPORT OR OPPOSITION IN PRIMARY

(1958 Legislative Candidates)

	Legislators		Defeated candidates	
Party action	Dem. (N = 54)	Rep. (N = 52)	Dem. (N = 52)	Rep. (N = 54)
	Percentage			
No competition	38.9	48.1	86.5	74.1
Party supported openly	42.6	36.5	5.8	9.3
Party supported covertly	7.4	5.8	5.8	9.3
Party divided	5.6	1.9	1.9	1.9
Party opposed openly	1.9	0	0	0
Party opposed covertly	0	3.8	0	1.9
No party action	3.7	3.8	0	1.9
No information	0	0	0	1.9

the *pro forma* support a party traditionally gives the incumbent, but in others it was given sufficiently early in the filing period to discourage other candidates from running. So, although party support in the uncontested primaries is not recorded in Table 23, one must recognize the potent, if immeasurable, deterrent power of a strong party endorsement in frightening off potential competition.

In the 1958 recruitment and selection process for the state legislature, consequently, the primary election constituted no real barrier to most of the candidates. Party supported most candidates, and a large majority of them (61.8 per cent) encountered no primary competition at all. Considerably more of the defeated candidates than the legislators were spared competition in the primary. The causes of that difference will be explored below.

When the candidates recalled their first candidacies for the legislature, they recalled considerably more party opposition to their initial candidacy than to the 1958 race; seventeen remembered initial party opposition, whereas only four reported it in 1958. Having been once defied and beaten, the parties accept and support the winner as long as he continues to seek the legislative seat. Whether in 1958 or earlier, this party opposition in the primary occurs in areas of likely party victory—where the nomination means election and is, therefore, worth fighting for. Party support in the primary, on the other hand, occurs chiefly in those strong and vital party organizations of both parties which recruit candidates and "police" the primary.

What difference does the candidate himself make in the party's decision on his aspirations? The incumbents get the greatest party support in the primary, and the longer the service the greater the likelihood of party endorsement, either covert or public, in the primary. Of the sixty-four candidates who received party help in the primary, twenty-four (37.5 per cent) had served in three or more sessions of the House; only 19 per cent of the other candidates facing primary competition in 1958 had logged that much legislative experience. Also, the longer the candidate has held party office, the greater the chance of positive party support in a primary contest. For instance, almost one-half the incumbents with at least five years of party officeholding had received party endorsement of their first candidacies, as against only 15.2 per cent of those with no record of party service.

What were the sources of the primary competition in 1958? At least half of the closest primary competitors were "independent" candidates running from personal motives without palpable party, factional, or nonpolitical group support. They were political loners for the most part, men driven by serious or frivolous motives to engage either an incumbent or a man with party support in a virtually hopeless fight. They ran to avenge some earlier party affront, to publicize their business or profession, to bring their political ambitions and vote-getting appeal to the attention of the party, or, in the case of some perennial candidates, out of some deep personal need for attention or notoriety. The next

105

most important source of primary competition was the dissident party faction. About a quarter of the closest primary competitors had some support from party factions not in control of the party hierarchy. Then, the party apparatus itself supported some primary losers in attempts to defeat the eventual winner. Also, the party may in a few instances have thrown into the primary fight dummy candidates whose only function was to divide the primary vote of the man or men challenging the party-supported candidate. Nonparty groups or elites supported almost none of the primary losers; we could uncover only five cases of such support among all the primary candidates who ran either second or third in the primary.

Party power and influence in these recruitment steps and maneuverings appear consistently as the indicators of party strength in Pennsylvania. Where the candidate himself has not originated the notion of seeking legislative office, the party has. Where encouragement and support has been given, the party or a party faction has given it. To be sure, the parties have not eliminated self-starting and independent candidacies—some party organizations have no intention of doing so—but they have shut other groups out of the recruitment process. Either they control the selection of candidates or no one does. In some districts, a candidate may indeed seek office independently to bring himself and his vote-getting ability to party attention. If he runs well, the party may "adopt" him and support him in the future. But, if he runs with nonparty or dissident party support, he has had the kiss of death.

The power of the parties in this process may be summarized by the candidates' estimates of whether their party had ever opposed their seeking election to the House. Had it ever tried to discourage them from running, inspired candidates against them, expressed displeasure with them, or supported primary opponents of theirs? Of the 212 candidates, 176 reported that they had never in their legislative candidacies been opposed by the party, and only twenty-eight (13.2 per cent) had impressions of party displeasure at some one of their candidacies. Compare this pattern with the one which Epstein reports for Wisconsin, an open-primary state given to a politics of independence and insurgency. More than half of his group of Wisconsin legislators reported winning original nomination when the party leaders were either opposed, neutral, or divided on their candidacy. Only one-fifth credited party leaders with originally suggesting they run for the state legislature, and only 27 per cent reported "encouragement" from party leaders and organization.[6]

Criteria of the Selection Process

The question of the criteria the parties apply in this recruitment and selection process may be approached from two directions. The criteria may be inferred from the social and political traits of the candidates. Chapter 4 dealt with those data and the inferences one may make from them. Or party leaders may be asked to identify the characteristics they seek in candidates for the legislature.[7] These two approaches to the question of criteria should, of course, show a high degree of correspondence. Especially in competitive constituencies, the effective party chairman will ideally be something of a virtuoso in picking candidates with the characteristics the voters of his district demand.

For at least 20 per cent of the parties of the state, the overriding criterion for the legislative candidate is simply the willingness to run as a sacrificial candidate. These minority parties offer him almost no chance of victory, and the chairman, as the party's talent scout, is usually in no position to be selective. He may even have to offer the potential candidate some inducement to enter the race—perhaps the promise of a patronage job. Frequently, the selection lights by default on particularly weak candi-

6. *Op. cit.,* p. 140.
7. This particular bit of information presents all the problems of constituency interviewing in exaggerated form. Informants often find it difficult to remember this sort of criterion, and, when they do, they often rationalize what was in reality no choice at all. Frequently the gap between the ideal criteria and the compromises which the party must make are great. Furthermore, the various leaders and wings of a party organization may pursue different criteria. Finally, local political leaders often find it difficult to verbalize this type of information; all too frequently they retreat into unintentional evasions—they seek, for instance, the "good man," the "winner," the "good vote-getter."

dates. One undermanned Republican organization, for example, was forced to accept a militant member of Protestants and Other Americans United for the Separation of Church and State for the 1958 race in a heavily Catholic, working-class district. The legislative spot on the party ticket is, indeed, one of the hardest for a minority party to fill. Whereas a minority party member may, through personal contacts and appeal, occasionally win local office, voting for the state legislative seat seems to be more strictly along party lines. To the politically ambitious, the race for the legislature appears the most nearly hopeless one in a one-party district.

At the other extreme, party leaders from the areas of sure victory, where the vote-getting qualities of the candidate may be fairly unimportant, search for the candidate loyal to the party and its leadership. They express their chief criteria in any number of ways—"service and hard work," "loyalty to the party," "support of the party leaders"—but they all boil down to party regularity and merit. In the words of one old party regular in the House, "They give you the House as something to work for, as a reward for service." The "they" needs no explanation. Of the eighteen Democratic legislators from Philadelphia who were interviewed, eight were Democratic ward leaders at the time of the 1958 elections, and all of the other ten were precinct committeemen or women. In Allegheny County, still a bastion of patronage, Democratic Party leaders not only scrutinize the prospective candidates' histories of party service, but also show a marked preference for candidates on the city or county payroll. Presumably the payrollers will, if elected, be more beholden to the party and more susceptible to party discipline. For the aggressive party organization which uses the legislative seat as elective patronage, service to the party remains the chief and logical test for aspirants.

Outside the cities and metropolitan areas, the parties of the homogeneous rural and small-town districts of the state seek candidates who bring to the ticket more general community esteem and recognition. Parties here seek the man of important organizational affiliations, higher education (preferably in law), and social status. They also, in the idiom of Pennsylvania politics, want a man with a "good name." That phrase combines under one rubric three separate and important components of "good name": the well-known name, the name of impeccable reputation, and the name of old and respected family ties. Politics in these districts tend to be personal, putting a premium on candidates known to the community. At least one party organization in the state begins its candidate recruitment by sifting through the membership lists of high-status fraternal and service organizations. And, where the party has a minority-party cast, its leadership may prefer the community leader for the very reason that he will not be identified with the party.

Beyond these partisan and electoral influences on candidate criteria, party recruiters must honor the standards the constituency itself sets down. The candidates must meet its expectations about age, sex, race, ethnic and religious background, occupation, social status, and roots in the community.[8] And it goes without saying that the ideal candidate will be personable, reasonably intelligent and able, and personally reputable. Not so long ago, a "two-terms-and-out" tradition prevailed in many of the districts of the state. The parties, recognizing the values of legislative seniority to themselves and the constituency, have in large part squelched that Jacksonian limit. But, in some of the poorer districts of the state, where public office remains something of a public benefice, tradition still supports the candidates who need the job—although just what constitutes "need" is difficult to say. Although this practice is on the wane, in a handful of depressed areas of the state resistance to candidates who already have a secure, well-paying job persists.

The art of ticket-balancing imposes an additional and complicating set of criteria on would-be candidates. Especially in the multimember districts and the larger, heterogeneous single-member districts, the social characteristics of the legislative candidates must be balanced either among themselves or with those of candidates for other local offices. If the district has identifiable

8. See Chapter 4.

areas or communities within it, it becomes necessary to pick candidates from the various geographic localities. In other constituencies, ethnic or religious groups may have to be propitiated. Party leaders mention the ethnic-religious consideration as the most important factor in ticket-balancing, with geographic distribution second; for the Republicans alone, however, geography ranks ahead of ethnic-religious considerations in recruiting candidates.

For the pragmatic political leader, the criteria he applies to candidate "timber" are not usually of his making. Aside from his varying insistence on party fidelity, he will observe the community-imposed criteria. The party chairman who dogmatically imposes personal criteria on candidates invites, in many instances, "principled defeat." Finally, for what it reaffirms about Pennsylvania politics, party leaders only infrequently mentioned ideological criteria for candidates. Either general ideological standards ("liberal" and "conservative") or those allied to party ("party principles" and the like) figured in the criteria listed by less than 10 per cent of the local party leaders interviewed. This selection system, should there be any lingering doubt, is not conducive to the emergence of ideologically oriented legislators in Pennsylvania.

Competitiveness of the Primary

Although the direct primary was devised to break the control of party caucuses over the selection of party candidates, it has also offered a substitute competition in the absence of close, two-party competition in the general election. Where one party dominates the politics of an area, the primary can, if it is competitive, offer a quasichoice for at least the voters of the majority party. But, in either of these two rationales for the primary, open and active competition remains the essential key to its successful operation. The competitiveness of a primary depends first of all on the number of candidates participating in it. But competition depends on more than sheer numbers of candidates. It rests on the ability of at least two to garner enough votes to be in real contention for the nomination.

In the primaries before the 1958 legislative elections, 204 of

110

the 308 primaries (66.2 per cent) went by default to the single candidate entered. In other words, in ninety-four Democratic (61 per cent) and 110 Republican primaries (71.4 per cent), there were no contests. In terms of candidates rather than districts, 123 Democrats (58.6 per cent) and 132 Republicans (62.8 per cent) —or 255 of 420 total candidates (60.7 per cent)—went into the November, 1958, general election without facing primary competition. Wisconsin, in the years 1946–1956, had contests in about 10 per cent more of the legislative primaries than did Pennsylvania.[9] But both states' experiences point to a rather stark absence of competition for the right to campaign for a seat in the state legislature.

A growing body of data and theory on state political systems suggests that primary competition is greater within the majority party and especially greater where the likelihood of victory in the general election is greatest. Just one exception exists to this generalization. In the areas of greatest party strength, competition falls off, but for reasons which are not at all clear. Perhaps these are the most homogeneous, unified, conforming areas or the ones with the strongest party organizations and the most electoral discipline. Although the incidence of primary competition appears to be chiefly a function of the prospects of election, two other factors—"ruralness" and incumbency—seem also to influence it. Primary competition declines in the rural areas and in those primaries in which incumbents are running.[10] The 1958 legislative primaries in Pennsylvania challenge these hunches and hypotheses in no major way.

The basic determinant of primary competition in Pennsylvania remains the prospect of victory in the election. As the percentage of Democratic vote in the subsequent election rises, competition in the Democratic primary increases, while that in the Republican primary diminishes (Table 24). And, as other studies have shown, competition diminishes in the parties' safest districts, those in which they polled more than 60 per cent of the legislative

9. Epstein, *op. cit.*, p. 131.
10. The bulk of this theory of primary competition comes from *ibid.*, pp. 131f., and Key, *American State Politics, op. cit.*, pp. 172f.

vote. Although one might logically expect that the presence of an incumbent in a party's primary would frighten off potential competitors, such is not the case. Competition tends to be greater in those districts in which incumbents run. Incumbents were present in 57.4 per cent of the contested Democratic primaries,

TABLE 24

RELATION BETWEEN PRIMARY COMPETITION AND
DEMOCRATIC VOTE IN THE 1958 ELECTION

Democratic percentage	Democratic primaries		Republican primaries	
	Contested (N = 61)	Not contested (N = 93)	Contested (N = 44)	Not contested (N = 110)
	Percentage			
0–39.9	3.3	20.4	22.7	10.0
40–49.9	13.1	41.9	36.4	28.2
50–59.9	42.6	16.1	31.8	24.5
60 and over	41.0	21.5	9.1	37.3

but in only 28 per cent of those without a contest. They ran in 68.2 per cent of the contested Republican primaries and in 48.2 per cent of the uncontested. The power of the incumbent cannot, apparently, offset the attractions of a majority party primary.[11]

It is no secret that the average party leader would gladly pass up the excitement of primary battles. They are expensive, they often inflict deep and slow-healing wounds, they take the eye of the party off the opposition, and they always threaten the possibility that the wrong man will win. But party organization apparently cannot overcome the factors which lead to competition

11. A "contested" primary is simply one that had more competitors than nominees to be chosen; a primary in a four-member district was considered contested if five men ran in it. The presence of a single incumbent in the race was sufficient to place it in the category of "incumbent present." In some of the multimember districts, though, there were fewer incumbents running than candidates to be nominated.

in the primary. The rate of contests is actually higher in the very primaries which are dominated by strong party organizations with a willingness to try, either openly or covertly, to influence their outcome (Table 25).[12] There is, of course, no way of knowing how many additional primary fights the endorsements of strong party organizations may have prevented, but the fact remains that primary contests take place, not only where expecta-

TABLE 25

RELATION BETWEEN COMPETITION IN THE PRIMARY
AND TYPE OF PARTY ORGANIZATION AND ACTION
IN PRIMARY

	Democratic primaries		Republican primaries	
	Contested (N = 28)	Not contested (N = 50)	Contested (N = 24)	Not contested (N = 54)
	Percentage			
Party organization				
A and B	75.0	38.0	50.0	22.2
C and D	25.0	62.0	50.0	77.8
Primary action				
Closed, covert	78.6	70.0	66.7	79.6
Open	21.4	30.0	33.3	20.4

tions of victory are greatest, but also where the party machinery is most virile.[13]

All this material suggests that primary competition arises from two factors: the likelihood of party victory in the constituency and the same political culture which produces the well-

12. The total numbers reported in tables 25 and 27 are smaller than in the other tables of this chapter because they deal of necessity with data from the interview sample rather than from all 154 legislative districts of the state.

13. This study was originally constructed to determine potential candidacies in the constituencies, but this line of questioning was abandoned after some notably unsuccessful trials. To determine the existence of candidacies that never really existed in any formal sense would probably demand more expertise in extrasensory perception than in political science.

organized parties. In the urban areas, a hyperpolitical way of life perhaps encourages people to seek rewards through political participation. No stigma attaches to frankly political motives and ambitions or even to their aggressive pursuit. In the less political constituencies, those of less primary competition, the very community pressures that stifle a forceful party apparatus, that make the vocation of the politician less than respectable, choke off candidacies that appear self-initiated or (even worse) self-serving. Leaving speculation aside, these data at the least caution against attributing the absence of primary competition to strength of party organization. The districts in which both the party itself and its chances for victory are the most feeble are those that offer the least competitive primaries.

Thus far we have been looking at a "competitiveness" defined by sheer number of contestants. Many of the premature conclusions one might reach about the incidence of primary competition are dispelled by looking at a second dimension of competition: the closeness of the primary races. A brief examination of the percentage differences in the contested primaries of the two parties reveals that the Democrats, though they had a greater number of contested primaries than the Republicans, also had many more contests that were virtually hopeless. In 34.4 per cent of Democratic primaries, as against 18.2 per cent of the Republican, the winner had a victory margin greater than 30 per cent of the votes cast. The total of contested primaries within the Democratic Party, then, is padded by futile races.

Of the 105 primaries contested in 1958, seventy-six (72.4 per cent) were decided by a margin of less than 30 per cent, a figure corresponding closely to Epstein's for Wisconsin in 1954 and 1956. There, about three-fourths of the primaries were decided by margins of less than two-to-one (33 per cent).[14] So, where primary

14. Epstein, *op. cit.*, p. 134. The Pennsylvania and Wisconsin data dispute Turner's findings that few primary contests for the U.S. House of Representatives were settled by margins of less than two-to-one. Julius Turner, "Primary Elections as the Alternative to Party Competition in 'Safe' Districts," *Journal of Policies*, XV (1953), No. 2, 197–210.

contests for the legislative nomination do exist in Pennsylvania, they usually involve more than merely token opposition.

Even though the number of contestants is greater in those primaries in which incumbents are running, the close primary races within the Democratic Party occur when no incumbents run (Table 26). The reverse is true in the Republican primaries. Furthermore, most of the close Democratic primary races occur where

TABLE 26

RELATION BETWEEN MARGIN OF PRIMARY VICTORY AND
PRESENCE OF INCUMBENT IN CONTESTED PRIMARIES

Margin of victory in primary	Democratic primaries		Republican primaries	
	With incumbent (N = 35)	Without incumbent (N = 26)	With incumbent (N = 30)	Without incumbent (N = 14)
Percentage	Percentage			
0–9.9	25.7	53.8	43.3	28.6
10–29.9	34.3	19.2	46.7	35.7
30 and over	40.0	26.9	10.0	35.7

the party organization has only moderate strength and does not intervene in the primary selection (Table 27). No such tendency can be observed in the Republican primaries. Finally, both parties experienced the closest primary races in areas of low Democratic general election vote—the Democrats where they lost, and the Republicans where they eventually won.

A brief recapitulation of this multitude of data on primary competition may be helpful. The situation in the Democratic primaries is clear. In sheer numbers, the greatest primary competition occurs in the areas of Democratic organizational and electoral strength, which are, of course, also the urban districts in which incumbents are likely to be running. But, on the other hand, the close races in the Democratic primaries occur in the districts of party weakness—weak organizations, few incumbents, and wan-

115

TABLE 27

RELATION BETWEEN MARGIN OF PRIMARY VICTORY AND
TYPE OF PARTY ORGANIZATION AND ACTION
IN PRIMARY

	Margin of victory in Democratic primaries			Margin of victory in Republican primaries		
	0–9.9	10–29.9	30 plus	0–9.9	10–29.9	30 plus
Party organization						
A and B	6	5	10	4	4	4
C and D	6	1	0	3	7	2
	12	6	10	7	11	6
Primary action						
Closed, covert	7	5	10	5	6	5
Open	5	1	0	2	5	1
	12	6	10	7	11	6

ing hopes of victory. Close races plague those Democratic organizations with no incumbents or party discipline to bring stability to the primary. The relationships in the Republican primaries are, unfortunately, not so clear. The Republicans, like the Democrats, reap the greatest number of primary contestants in districts of their electoral strength (the districts in which they would also naturally have incumbents). But they tend much more than do the Democrats to have their close primary races in the same districts. Two factors may explain the difference. Since the Republicans simply have fewer hopeless primary fights, any distinctions based on the closeness of the Republican primary are less significant. Second, and perhaps more important, the Republicans stage many of their contests in the rural districts, in which no strong party discipline and no political culture of party regularity exist to support the will of the party.

⟨ *The 1958 General Elections*

It has been remarked that the state representative's role is marked by dependence on the capricious, unpredictable turns of

state and national elections.[15] To a great extent, the state legislator does win or lose in a game of political roulette over which
he sets no odds. The Pennsylvania legislative elections of 1956, influenced as they were by the Eisenhower landslide, upset many
budding legislative careers. The 1958 elections were, however, isolated from the great fluctuations of two years before. It was the
year for the election of a governor and a United States senator—
one of which each party won narrowly.

As the culmination of this recruitment and selection process,
the 1958 elections offered the final point at which party and voter
choice could be expressed. But in many of the legislative contests the voters had little or no realistic choice. So entrenched is
one or the other party in many legislative constituencies that possibilities for effective competition are painfully remote. If one accepts the 40–60 per-cent range as "competitive," then eighty-eight
districts, electing 120 of the 210 representatives, fall within the
range of competition.[16] By this definition, 57.1 per cent of the 154
elections to the House qualify. But a 60–40 per-cent, or 58–42-
vote, division is hardly competitive by the standards of fine-line
party competitiveness which reckon a 56 per-cent presidential
vote as a landslide. So, adopting a 45–55 per-cent spread as a truer
test of competition, only fifty districts (32.5 per cent) met this
criterion; in 1956, only forty-four constituencies met it. In two
of the districts, competition shrank to nothing in 1958. In both,
the Republican nomination went begging, the incumbent Democrat won it with a few unsolicited write-in votes, and then both
Democrats beat themselves at the general election.

If one treats the primary and general elections together as a
single electoral system, he can estimate their cumulative competitiveness. In just twenty Democratic and twenty-one Republican
constituency parties did the respective voters enjoy some choice

15. Duncan MacRae, "The Role of the State Legislator in Massachusetts,"
American Sociological Review, XIX (1954), No. 2, 185.
16. Because of the multimember districts, figures used here must be for
districts rather than candidates; in the multimember districts, margins of
candidates on a base of 100 per cent are impossible to compute. The vote
percentages for the party's candidates in each constituency consist here of the
sum of the vote percentage of the party's individual candidates.

in the primary and a general election vote within the 55–45 per-cent range. If one applies that 10 per-cent range to primary as well as general elections, only seventeen of the 308 constituency parties (against only eleven in 1956) qualify as presenting the voters with two truly competitive choices. Perhaps more signifi-cantly, in only sixty-three Democratic parties and in sixty Repub-lican parties (a total of 39.9 per cent) did the voters have a close contest (10 per-cent range) in either the primary or the general election. In 1956, it was a similar 38.6 per cent.

To look at competitiveness from the other extreme, in sixty-three Democratic and eighty-one Republican parties in 1958, the voters had neither a contested primary nor a general election con-test within the 10 per-cent competitive range. That means that, in 46.8 per cent of the constituency parties, whoever recruited the party's candidate probably made the only meaningful choice in the entire process.

Who Recruits?

To think of the process by which we select representatives in terms of formal elections is to miss the subtlety of the selection process. In Pennsylvania, two cardinal facts stand out. Given the limited competitiveness of the primaries and general elections in many districts of the state, the effective and crucial selection is made informally before the primary and general elections. Sec-ond, if any agency other than the candidates themselves per-form that recruitment and selection function, it is the political party.

In Pennsylvania, the political party dominates the candidate and legislator selection system. In addition to exercising its classic role in the general election, it intervenes freely in the primary elections and supervises the preprimary recruiting activities. Yet, even so powerful a party system as Pennsylvania's does not move without limits or difficulties. In setting criteria for the candidates it recruits, it cannot fail to observe the canons of acceptability which the constituency establishes. Although it may be able to control the primary, all of its power has been unable to choke off competition there. The pattern of two-party competition con-

118

tinues to influence the numbers of would-be legislators who flock to the primaries.

And what limits has the direct primary imposed on the party selection role? In Pennsylvania, the parties have not had to resort to elaborate preprimary caucuses or even, in many instances, to formal preprimary endorsements. Nor has the state seen the rise of extraparty organizations to re-establish discipline in the primary. Plainly, Pennsylvania parties, strong and vital by any standard, have not been greatly discomfited by the primary. In fact, one can reasonably argue that they have turned it to their purposes by making it another hurdle for the unanointed candidate. The primary's multiplication of campaigning and expense, its sheer institutional complexity, and its unstable patterns of competition can only discourage the lonely candidate. The very party organizations which the primary was created to break, the strong and vigorous organizations, are those most capable of turning the primary to their uses.

Where the parties have not mastered the primary, nonparty groups have controlled it. Parties, for their part, have any number of reasons for wanting to keep the selection process out of the primary—reasons having to do with such crucial matters as party finance, internal cohesion, success at the general election, and the loyalty of candidates and officeholders. These concerns, needless to say, touch the very health and success of the party. To control the primary is for them often a matter of survival. In Pennsylvania, that challenge has been well met. The parties have reasserted themselves as nominators.

Unanswered here are the questions of the degree to which the party elites—those who select the candidates—coincide with the social and economic elites of the community and the extent to which they all coincide with the officeholding groups. In the small-town and rural areas of Pennsylvania, there is considerable overlap among these various groups. There, the line between party and nonparty groups—even in the selection function—is indistinct in the great homogeneity and consensus that colors community political life. The pressures of the dominant social and economic groups of the community are felt as much *in* the

119

party as *on* it. In these areas, furthermore, the legislative district often approximates the local community, and active participation in politics tends to be of itself participation in the affairs of the community and its elites. The contrary is true of selection in urban and metropolitan areas. The urban constituency tends to be only a fragment of the community. The party tends to be rooted in a specific religious, occupational, ethnic, or economic group which may bear little relation to the more powerful elites of the city.

So, contrary to the experience of other states,[17] the political party in Pennsylvania exercises enormous control over the business of picking state legislators. It has been able to absorb the direct primary into its domination of the selection process, and it has largely been able to exclude nonparty groups from significant influence in it. It has, in other words, established the type of party control over the election and pre-election steps in picking legislative representatives which we associate with programmatic, disciplined, "responsible" political parties.

17. Contrast the Pennsylvania party role, decribed in this chapter, with that of the parties in Oregon. Lester G. Seligman, in "Party Roles and Political Recruitment," *Western Political Quarterly*, XI (1958), No. 2, 361, reports that "party per se plays almost no role [in recruitment]—its role in nominating is shared or substituted by [a] variety of groups. . . ."

6 • Legislative Roles and Votes

      While scholars argue leisurely over the sources of the elected representative's responsibility, the legislator is forced by his office to solve the problem virtually every day of his tenure. The need to balance the demands of his party, his constituency, and those guides he has within himself is as real as the certainty of an election in a few years and as intimately tied to his political future.

      The legislature itself presents the final opportunity for the party to enter the representational process. It is there that the party tests its relationship with its elected candidates and tries to establish their responsibility to a party program. In Pennsylvania, the parties have achieved not only an active level of party organization, but a sizable role before and during the primary recruitment process. By all counts, they have met the recruiting conditions necessary for discipline within the legislature. This chapter examines the final fruits of those efforts.

The Legislator in the Mirror

In 1938, *Fortune* magazine approached a sample of the American electorate with the question: "Do you believe that a congressman should vote on any question as the majority of his constituents desire, or vote according to his own judgment?" More than 54 per cent of the respondents chose "his own judgment," and more than 37 per cent declared for the constituency. The remainder offered no opinion.[1] Some twenty years later, a team of political scientists questioning the legislators themselves in four states found that 63 per cent identified themselves with a "trustee" role very similar to *Fortune*'s "own-judgment" alternative.[2]

The results of these two studies illustrate the problem of defining the legislative role. They indicate that a majority of both governors and governed formally subscribe to the image of the legislator as a free, unfettered decision-maker, drawing his wisdom chiefly, if not completely, from his own virtue, knowledge, and experience. The vernacular of our politics has, in fact, a series of unflattering epithets for the legislator who has surrendered that independent spirit to either party or constituency. He is a "cat's-paw," a "rubber stamp," a "lackey." Given this attitude, no dispute, one assumes, could rage here between a Burke and his Bristol. Yet do these formal protestations reflect the real expectations of constituents and of legislators? Most legislators know too well how quickly their constituents turn against them when they differ from their representative's "independent" judgment. Formal attributions of role aside, they must conjure with the demands and scrutiny of their electors.

To determine their solution to the cross-pressures of constitu-

1. "The Fortune Survey," *Fortune*, XVIII (1938), No. 5, 96; quoted in Alfred de Grazia, *Public and Republic* (New York: A.A. Knopf, 1951), p. 158.
2. Heinz Eulau, John Wahlke, William Buchanan, and Leroy Ferguson, "The Role of the Representative: Some Empirical Observations on the Theory of Edmund Burke," *American Political Science Review*, LIII (1959), No. 3, 742–756. The authors break the legislative role into two dimensions, one of "style" focus (trustee, delegate, and politico), the other of "area" focus (district, state, district-plus-state). However, the delegate in style coincides, as one might expect, with the district-area focus. He directs his responsibilities to the district which chose him rather than to the state as a whole.

ency, party, and personal commitment, the Pennsylvania legislative candidates of this study were asked several open-ended questions about their legislative role.[3] On the basis of their extended responses, they were categorized three times: once on their resolution of the district-wishes–versus–own-judgment conflict, once by the degree of party loyalty expressed, and once by their general ranking of constituency, party, and own judgment in their overall concept of the legislative role. Table 28 reports the general results.

Contrary to the four-state study mentioned above, only 31.1 per cent of the Pennsylvania legislative candidates declared clearly for their personal judgment (the trustee role) in the event of its conflict with their constituents' wishes. Even when one takes only those candidates who chose a clear alternative, the percentage of trustees rises to only 45.8. The discrepancy between these two studies may be explained on several grounds. The localism that ties a legislator to his constituents flourishes in Pennsylvania, more widely perhaps than in comparable states. "Servicing the constituents" absorbs an important part of every legislator's attention. The representative with pockets full of driver's-license applications for his personal processing is not an uncommon sight in the General Assembly. Many legislative campaigns are fought on the issue of what the incumbent legislator did or did not "get" for the district in the two years of his stewardship. Every errand run in Harrisburg, every patronage job garnered for a constituent, every road paved or repaved in the district scores valuable points in the home town or county. The strength of these local demands may reflect the heightened needs of the failing and depressed sectors of the state. Like the feverish demands for patronage, they may reflect the politics of declining prosperity in which the benefits of the state assume a growing importance. And, like the de-

3. The three opening questions were: "Do you think a legislator should be primarily guided by the wishes of his district, of his party, or by his own judgment?" "What should he do if his district wants one thing, and he believes in another?" "How much loyalty do you think a legislator owes his party?" They were often followed by additional clarifying and probing questions.

TABLE 28

EXPRESSIONS OF LEGISLATIVE ROLE BY 1958
LEGISLATIVE CANDIDATES *

	Legislators		Defeated candidates	
	Dem. (N = 54)	Rep. (N = 52)	Dem. (N = 52)	Rep. (N = 54)
	Percentage			
I. Constituency versus judgment				
Constituency ("delegate")	35.2	42.3	30.8	38.9
Own judgment ("trustee")	40.7	25.0	34.6	24.1
Compromise, evasion	24.1	30.8	32.7	18.5
No information	0	1.9	1.9	18.5
II. Degree of party loyalty				
Hostile, weak	5.6	7.7	15.4	25.9
Moderate	48.1	57.7	59.6	46.3
Strong	42.6	28.8	19.2	9.3
No information	3.7	5.8	5.8	18.5
III. General role				
Party-oriented	11.1	5.8	3.8	1.9
District-oriented	35.2	55.8	34.6	38.9
Self-oriented	31.5	19.2	40.4	29.6
None discernible	22.0	17.3	19.2	11.1
No information	0	1.9	1.9	18.5

* For further explanation of the categories used here, see Appendix "B."

mands for patronage, they reflect a political style built on immediate, direct rewards to the participants.

The lower incidence of "trustees" in Pennsylvania may also
reflect the complex and equivocating answers these questions
elicited. A number asserted that conflicts between their districts
and their judgments were rare. "A man usually agrees with his
district, since he's one of them and typical of them," one legislator noted. Another reported that his main problem was in

getting any response—even one of opposition—from his urban district: "It's hard to get them to think about anything happening down here in Harrisburg." Others whisked the problem away with a little semantic trickery. "A representative's judgment," according to one, "should arise from knowing the needs and wants of his district and state." The choice between district and personal judgment is an artificial issue for many legislators. They have no really clear or elaborate ideological guides or thought-out positions which encumber them as they decide between a "yea" and a "nay." Furthermore, they are so much creatures of their constituencies that they share its goals and values fully. The value of this classic dilemma in representative theory may, in other words, be chiefly heuristic.

Just where party fits into legislative choice in Pennsylvania appears to be, by the candidates' wishes, a separable problem. When confronted with the question of party as against constituency and own judgment as sources of legislative responsibility, only two (one incumbent of each party) of the 200 responding legislators chose party. Doubtless the social, and even political, unacceptability of such a response was crucial. Certainly, this virtually unanimous unwillingness to admit the guidance of party stands at odds with the considerable amount of party discipline in the Pennsylvania legislature. And, since that discipline (discussed later in this chapter) is greater among the Democrats, one may wonder whether their preference for personal judgment over district guidance might not mask commitments to party.

In identifying their own degree of party loyalty, many candidates and legislators saw no great conflict between party and their commitment to constituency and self. The party to which they pledge fealty is usually the local constituency party, a semiautonomous political barony sensitive to the desires of its constituents. Its main concerns are local improvements and patronage, and it is only rarely stirred to support a state-wide party program or gubernatorial administration. Also widespread among the interviewees was a purely pragmatic approach to party loyalty— one supports the party to the degree necessary to win the party's electoral support and to the degree to which that support is crucial for victory. Any number of rural legislators explained their tenuous ties to party simply in terms of the party's doing little for them at election-time.

We have thus far assumed that the legislators' choices reflect the threefold pressures of party, constituency, and self. To put it that baldly, of course, overlooks the complexity of these three sources of legislative responsibility. Constituency party may conflict with legislative party, and the legislator's loyalties to his occupational interest may contradict his awareness of those broader interests which he calls "the public interest" in his statesmanlike moments.

The average legislator appears, then, to make no firm commitment to constituency, party, or self. Their demands on him and their sanctions over him shift from issue to issue. Both the shifting political demands and the finely balanced equities of choice force him to choose only tentatively and cautiously, one issue at a time. Yet, there is a handful of legislators and defeated candidates who approach that artificial construct, the pure type, and who vest their legislative responsibility almost exclusively in one of the three sources. Small though their number is, they afford useful illustrations in human terms of the three extreme dimensions of the legislative role. A composite and fictional picture of each, based largely on two or three cases, follows.

Rep. George Williams, the "delegate" par excellence, is as closely wedded to his legislative constituency as any man in Harrisburg. Catering to its every fleeting wish has been the story of his legislative career. His constituency—a homogeneous, somewhat provincial farming county in the central section of the state —adheres to a traditional two-party politics having little about them of the ideological currents of the past thirty years. It draws party lines largely along old family and clan lines, and it expects only that a state legislator tend to local demands. Williams, a merchant whose business keeps him in contact with the rural folks of the county, does exactly that. "I know I've done more for my people than any other representative this county has ever had," he proclaims proudly. "I've found out what they wanted and tried to get it for them." Fairly wealthy by local standards,

126

he has few organizational memberships in the county seat and has little truck with social circles there. His ties are closer to the out-county people, to whom he is a fixer, friend, patron, and confidant. He is especially adept in finding patronage jobs in Harrisburg for the people of the county (regardless of party), and he willingly intercedes with distant authority (such as the Bureau of Motor Vehicles) when it threatens a local resident. On a somewhat broader scale, Williams works tirelessly to bring light industry into the county to offset the decline in farm production. His political success may be marked by the fact that he has won four terms in the House, breaking the tradition of "two terms and out" for the county's legislator. His political success has naturally made him a power in his party's county committee, but party remains for him at best a concerted expression of the wishes of the constituency.

The errand-boy role, however, holds little appeal for Rep. John Gibbons. Although his constituency is not so completely rural as Williams', it is not vastly different. Gibbons, however, is an *idéologue* and the epitome of the "trustee" in legislative affairs. In an interview, his voice tends to rise, and his speech inclines to finger-poking, conversational oratory. "We've gotten too far away from principle—government and politics are too expedient—too much giving away and too many promises to get votes. We need a new set of guiding principles." His principles, however, are general, moralistic, and nonpolitical: running government "like a big business," reforming the laws and the constitution of the state, getting "the incompetents" (apparently the patronage holders) out of state government. In his county, he maintains a law practice and active community ties—the Rotary, Little League, and the Masons. And yet he resists constituency pressures with the conviction that the majority is not always right and that the legislator must above all not yield his "conscience" to any man. Only the fact that he, as a lifelong resident of the county, is so steeped in its needs and values saves him from disastrous independence. As it is, grumbling mounts within the county about his inattention to mail and phone calls, and many voters can tick off the last, distant year in which a new road was built in the county.

127

To his party he accords only an uncertain loyalty. "I won't wear the party chains like many in the House," he claims.

Belonging to an even rarer species, the unalloyed "partisan," Frank Naughton represents two thickly settled metropolitan wards. In a lower-middle-class ward in which first- and second-generation Irish Catholics predominate, he is a lifelong resident and an Irish Catholic. He has worked as a precinct committeeman for seventeen years, and since his election to the House some seven years ago he has been a ward leader. His father had earlier been active in local politics for more than twenty-five years, and Naughton today thrives, as his father did, amid the intricate, Byzantine convolutions of the urban political machine. His friends come exclusively from the party and from the labor-union circles to which his sometime occupation as a tool-and-die–maker gives him access. The world of social and fraternal organizations attracts him very little. His role as faithful party follower is, then, not unexpected. The party organization tapped him as a candidate for the legislature, although he had never before run for public office, and the party vote elected him and continues to elect him to the House. "They [the party]," he explains, "have the greatest insight into the wishes of the district. I owe them 100 per-cent loyalty—I wouldn't be here if it wasn't for the party." This is not to say, though, that Naughton is inattentive to his constituents or even to the general interests of labor and the common man. He serves them through service to the party.

Atypical though Williams, Gibbons, and Naughton are, they represent the three "legislators" who battle for recognition within every member of the House. Peculiarities of constituency and their personal ideologies have made it possible for them to choose one of the three with unusual certainty and consistency. But to a greater degree, their single course or role is but a verbalism, a recognition that, for them, at least two of the three options frequently coincide. The man of little education and even less experience in formulating ideologies and in whose constituency party organization is little more than a local booster club can, for instance, opt for the single role of "delegate" with few qualms and considerable impunity.

128

Legislative Role

Since the legislator's concepts of his responsibility and of his role as a representative define and guide his work in the House, their importance for the legislative process needs no elaboration. But how does one explain the differing concepts? Do active local party organizations, for example, produce party-oriented legislators, or do these partisans emerge from other party systems? Does legislative role reflect personal or general social experience, or perhaps previous legislative service or other public officeholding?

Turning back to the choice between constituency and personal judgment, we see that both victorious and defeated Republicans profess greater willingness to follow the constituency's guide than do the Democrats (Table 28). Virtually no differences appear within either party between the winners and the losers of 1958. But why the party differences? The answer, frankly, is not clear.

Years of experience in the House itself count for little in the establishment of legislative role among the incumbents. But, among the Democratic winners, the "delegates'" affinity for district guidance is related to years of service in the party apparatus. The median length of party service of the "delegates" in the Democratic Party was five years, whereas for the "trustees" it was none. Among the Republican legislators, it was two years to none. Despite this relationship between party service and the "delegate's" role, it makes no difference in what type of party that service was given. In the area of personal backgrounds and histories, few clues emerge. College graduates and holders of advanced degrees, especially within the Democratic ranks, tend away from district allegiance and toward legislative independence. But, beyond these shreds of data, no firm explanations of the incidence of "trustees" and "delegates" appear.

Hasty answers, poor questions, or misinterpretation of the responses may be at fault. There may be a number of systems conditioning the acquisition of legislative role. Personal observation suggests that differing assumptions about the political role,

129

themselves the product of more general political cultures, may prevail in urban and rural areas of the state. The influence of party may help clarify role choice. Where the candidate has been close to a strong and successful party apparatus, the political sensitivity to constituents that is the essence of the political craft may lure him from the nonpartisan values of the unfettered "trustee." In sum, though, the mechanics of this part of the education of the legislator must on these data be recorded as a mystery.

On the assumption that the "delegate's" cultivated attentiveness to the district reflects a political localism, some data on other expressions of localism may offer clues to the political role of the delegate. Each legislative candidate, winner and loser alike, was asked in the interview what three issues he stressed most heavily in the 1958 election campaign. (Not all mentioned three; some, in fact, were unable, four to nine months later, to remember a single one. That fact in itself says a great deal about legislative politics in Pennsylvania.) On the basis of these responses, two groups of candidates were defined: those who mentioned one or more issues oriented to the local constituency, and those who mentioned none.[4]

These two groups of candidates reflect important constituency differences. Those who ran pledged to new roads or dams or industry for the district come slightly more often than the other candidates from the rural, sparsely populated centers of the state. The urban constituencies are not very often the self-contained communities in which local issues and needs can be framed. Here, too, party loyalty and partisan issues make greater demands on the legislative candidate. Not surprisingly, then, the candidate who capitalizes on the local issue more frequently comes from the district of weak party organization and loose party control of the primary. One-third of the local-issue proponents came from parties which maintain the open primary; only 18.8 per

---

4. A listing of "local" and "nonlocal" issues is to be found in Appendix "B."

cent of the adherents of more general issues came from similar parties.

There is, however, no real connection between this localism of issue and the localism of the legislator who dons the mantle of "delegate." Those legislators running on local issues show only a little more inclination to the "delegate's" role than do those who ran on nonlocal issues. The choice between "delegate" and "trustee" roles is evidently caught up in both urban-rural differences and differences in party strength. At least in rural areas, the association of the trustee role with the well-organized party is clear; 39.3 per cent of the trustees and only 6.1 per cent of the delegates from the rural districts come from "A" and "B" type parties. Few such differences prevail in the urban districts. In these city districts, party and constituency pressures may be more compatible, permitting the legislator to express party loyalty through loyalty to the constituency. All of this is, however, conjecture. The complexities of these role choices escape the data and analysis of this study.

The roots of party orientation and party loyalty are, fortunately, not so fully hidden. A stronger party loyalty marks legislators than defeated candidates (Table 28). The experience of the legislative session, especially those as sharply divided as recent ones in Pennsylvania, reinforces party loyalties. The recent sessions impress, too, the dangers and wrath one courts by bucking the party caucus. Few members of the House had forgotten the 1958 primary purge of two Pittsburgh Democrats who had refused in the 1957 session to support the governor's fiscal program. Party, too, makes itself indispensable for the legislator by guiding him in the ways of legislating and by clarifying the confusing jumble of choices confronting him. Powerful party caucuses and apparatuses create their own rationale and their own loyalists.

The legislative party, in addition, profits from the transfer of loyalties from constituency parties. Protestations of fealty to the party came from those candidates who were the product of strong party organizations (Table 29). Whether one divides the candidates by party or by victory and failure in 1958, the picture remains the same. The degree of loyalty the candidate gives the party is greater among those from strong party organizations and from parties active in the preprimary and primary recruitment chores. Naturally, then, party loyalty among Democrats out-

TABLE 29

RELATION BETWEEN DEGREE OF PARTY LOYALTY AND TYPE OF PARTY ORGANIZATION AND ACTION IN PRIMARY

	Democrats			Republicans		
	Degree of party loyalty			Degree of party loyalty		
	Weak (N = 11)	Moderate (N = 57)	Strong (N = 33)	Weak (N = 18)	Moderate (N = 55)	Strong (N = 20)
	Percentage					
Party organization						
A and B	18.2	43.9	78.8	27.8	32.7	65.0
C and D	81.8	56.1	21.2	72.2	67.3	35.0
Primary action						
Closed, covert	36.4	77.2	87.9	61.1	83.6	75.0
Open	63.6	22.8	12.1	38.9	16.4	25.0

stripped that among Republicans (Table 28). Since the Democrats tend to stronger, more aggressive organizations in the constituencies, they have more local organizational loyalty to convert into discipline within the legislative party. As the majority party in the legislature—and one working with a precariously slim majority at that—the Democrats may also have keenly felt the need to rally behind a legislative program and a Democratic governor.

Inconclusive though they may be, these self-evaluations of legislative role do scotch one old and one recent suggestion about legislative role. No evidence here supports the recent proposition that representatives now increasingly define their job in the "trustee" dimension because constituent control over their activities is increasingly thwarted by the intricacy and obscurity of contemporary governmental issues.[5] Party and constituency influences remain potent in Pennsylvania, and in adopting a posture as an elected representative the members of the House acknowledge that fact. Even as issues of public policy become forbiddingly complex for the citizen, so do they also for the only slightly more experienced state legislator. He may be increasingly happy to accept the cues and leadership of an all-knowing party or of knowledgeable constituents. Since the average state legislator legislates only as a part-time, semiprofessional representative, competing policy alternatives may confuse and confound him as readily as they do his constituents.

Nor does this study lend any support to the old argument, propounded by Bryce and Luce among others, that multiple-member districts will counteract and offset the localism and "peanut politics" of single-member districts.[6] They argue that the single representative is more vulnerable than the representatives of a multimember district to the concentrated wrath of any interest or faction he offends. One could as plausibly argue, however, that the two or three legislators from one district constantly face the threat of being divided, compared, and played off against one another. But, impressions and logical plausibility aside, no differences in legislative attitude or role appear in Pennsylvania between candidates from the single-member and those from multimember districts.

Party Cohesion and Responsibility

Given the decentralized, nonideological character of the two American parties, "party responsibility" in American legislatures

---

5. Eulau *et al.*, *op. cit.*, among others, make this point.

6. This argument is well summarized by Maurice Klain, "A New Look at the Constituencies: The Need for a Recount and a Reappraisal," *American Political Science Review*, XLIX (1955), No. 4, 1118. See also Harold F. Gosnell, *Democracy*, "The Threshold of Freedom" (New York: Ronald Press, 1948), p. 172.

has been notably difficult to establish. Responsibility assumes the ability of the parties to articulate a clear program. Voters may then select the candidates of one or the other party with the confidence that the party of the majority will enact its proposals into public policy. Especially within the legislative chambers, the majority party must display the internal discipline necessary to carry out its pre-election commitments. In the legislature, then,

> party government requires the existence of parties which have sufficient coherence and discipline for their members to display solidarity on all great questions of public policy. After all, party government is based upon the substitution of *party* for individual responsibility. If the members of each party frequently desert their party's line on questions of public policy, then the people cannot effectively either blame or reward either party, *as a party*, for what it does or does not do.[7]

Only through the single agency of the political party is the legislator able to establish contact with and responsibility to his constituency. The three sources of responsibility—party, constituency, and self—merge into one: the "responsible" party.

Although discipline and cohesion among legislators of the same party do not by themselves guarantee party responsibility, they are its necessary conditions. The proclivity of legislators to cross party lines has balked the achievement of greater responsibility. The blame for the softness of party lines ultimately falls back on the close, personal dependence of the legislator on his constituents. Any legislator or candidate who can carry the primary may, despite his party's distaste for him, succeed even as a party maverick.

The extent to which party loyalties count in American legislatures differs dramatically, depending on both the locale of the legislature and the method of measuring party discipline. Using the chi-square test on party alignments in roll calls in the House

7. Austin Ranney, *The Doctrine of Responsible Party Government*, "Its Origins and Present State" (Urbana: University of Illinois Press, 1954), p. 16. Emphasis in the original.

of Representatives, Julius Turner found significant party influence in nearly 90 per cent of the Congressional roll calls he examined.[8] Lockard's study of the Connecticut legislature also
found a strikingly high degree of party cohesion, this time in the
legislature of a state with vigorous party politics. Over a six-ses-
sion span in the Connecticut legislature, the Democrats achieved
average cohesion indexes of 80.9, 86.8, 87.3, 83.9, 99.7, and 52.1
per cent in the lower house. The Republicans averaged 76.6, 80.0,
84.0, 77.3, 99.0, and 74.5 per cent.[9] Over the six sessions, then,
the Democrats reached a median a little over 80 per cent, the
Republicans a little under it. Lockard ascribes this party discipline to the organizational strength of the Connecticut parties
(which at the time were still operating without the direct primary), their competitiveness, their ideological differences, and
their determined efforts to enforce party divisions in the state
legislature.[10] Using the same index, Turner found an average
party cohesion in the House of Representatives in 1944 of 70.8
per cent for the Republicans and 56 for the Democrats.[11]

There is no constitutional requirement to record roll calls
on every issue in Connecticut, and Lockard's index is based on
session totals of between four and fourteen roll calls. Very likely,
these votes were recorded at least in part because one party or both
chose to make a record on them. In Pennsylvania, the legislators
must record their votes on all bills passed, and the record of
party alignments on all bills passed is complete. In studying party

8. Turner, *Party and Constituency,* "Pressures on Congress" (Baltimore:
The Johns Hopkins Press, 1951), p. 29. The measure of significance here is
the chi-square test, where $P = 1/100$. That is to say, in 90 per cent of the
roll calls Turner examined, the chances that the observed division of
partisans on opposite sides of the vote would occur by chance is less than
one in a hundred.

9. This index is the one associated with Stuart Rice and is computed
by dividing the party's deviating minority by all its members and then con-
verting the percentage (which will of necessity be no smaller than 50) to a
scale from 0 to 100. Stuart Rice, *Quantitative Methods in Politics* (New York:
Knopf, 1928).

10. W. Duane Lockard, "Legislative Politics in Connecticut," *American
Political Science Review,* XLVIII (1954), No. 1, 166–173.

11. *Op. cit.,* p. 27.

PARTY AND REPRESENTATION

discipline in the 1951 session of the Pennsylvania legislature, Keefe found initially that the overwhelming number of roll-call votes was unanimous; 927 of 1,330 roll calls in the House (69.7 per cent) showed not a single dissent. In another 228 (17.1 per cent), majorities of both parties were in agreement on the proposal before the House; in 175 (13.2 per cent), majorities of the parties opposed each other. Using Lowell's standard of "party vote" (at least 80 per cent of one party versus at least 80 per cent of the other), Keefe found only 10.7 per cent party votes. In the state Senate, he found only 4.7 per cent. Noting the high degree of unanimity and party concurrence, Keefe concluded that the Pennsylvania legislature had "not a very significant amount of party conflict." [12] Earlier, Keefe had found that, in two sessions of the Illinois General Assembly, party votes never exceeded 4.4 per cent.[13] Using the Lowell standard, Lockard computed the percentage of party votes in Connecticut from 50 to 90.[14]

Clearly, in using either the Rice or the Lowell measures of party conflict, the crucial question is the part of total legislative work reflected in the roll calls recorded. In the 1959 session of the Pennsylvania House of Representatives, 1,738 roll calls were recorded, and 934 of these (53.7 per cent) were unanimous. In another 571 (32.8 per cent), majorities of the two parties voted together, leaving only 235 votes (13.5 per cent) in which majorities of the two parties voted on opposing sides. But discipline, even the kind on which party responsibility is to be built, means something more than cohesion on party votes. It demands that parties maintain cohesion on an issue even when they agree substantially. On the 804 nonunanimous votes in the House, the Democrats achieved 80 per-cent cohesion on 718 of them (89.3 per cent), the Republicans on 671 (83.5 per cent). In comparing this figure with the Rice index which Lockard uses, one must

12. William Keefe, "Parties, Partisanship, and Public Policy in the Pennsylvania Legislature," *American Political Science Review,* XLVIII (1954), No. 2, 452.
13. "Party Government and Lawmaking in the Illinois General Assembly," *Northwestern University Law Review,* XLVII (1952), No. 1, 55–71.
14. *Op. cit.,* p. 170.

136

remember that these data mean that the Pennsylvania parties would show a cohesion index over 60 per cent in more than four of every five votes.

The incidence of party discipline may, however, be shown by other than aggregate data on roll calls. The individual legislator's adherence to his party majority serves as an index of personal loyalty. In the 1959 Pennsylvania House, none of the Democrats and only seven Republicans voted against the majority of their fellow partisans in 20 per cent or more of the nonunanimous roll calls (Table 30). In terms of discipline or adherence to the party majority, rather than in terms of opposition in party votes, one may say conservatively that Pennsylvania's legislators display notable party discipline.

The beginning of an explanation of party discipline among Pennsylvania legislators fairly leaps from Table 30. The majority Democrats evince a vastly greater party cohesion than do the Republicans. Regardless of the type of issue—parties in agreement or parties in opposition—the Democrats consistently display the greater discipline. That difference between parties undoubtedly reflects the chief organizational problem of the session: the struggle of the Democrats, as the majority party, to mobilize 106 of their 108 members for the absolute majority required of all legislation. With this small a majority, the Democrats could tolerate few, if any, defections, and pressure on Democratic members throughout the session was unrelenting. The governor and the Democratic leadership could and did use the state patronage as both whip and carrot.

The Republicans, by contrast, were a large, heterogeneous minority under no pressure to enact any program of legislation. This is not to suggest, however, that cohesion will necessarily be greater in the party of the majority. The considerable Democratic cohesion in this case probably reflects the needs of the majority party in a closely divided chamber. If the party division in the House were lopsided, the majority party, operating with a luxurious margin, might tolerate a significant number of deviations. And the small, homogeneous minority corps might find itself inclining toward—and driven to—a disciplined resistance.

137

TABLE 30

DEVIATIONS FROM PARTY MAJORITIES BY LEGISLATORS OF EACH PARTY ON VARIOUS TYPES OF ROLL CALL *

	Types of roll call									
	Majorities in agreement		Majorities opposed; one or both less than 80 per-cent cohesion		"Party votes"; majorities opposed; each at 80 per-cent cohesion		All roll calls with party majorities in opposition		All nonunanimous roll calls	
Deviation Percentage	Dem. (N=108)	Rep. (N=102)	Dem. (N=108)	Rep. (N=102)	Dem. (N=108)	Rep. (N=102)	Dem. (N=108)	Rep. (N=102)	Dem. (N=108)	Rep. (N=102)
					Percentage					
0–4	67.6	8.8	13.0	2.0	71.3	47.1	32.4	2.9	54.6	2.0
5–9	32.4	42.2	29.6	1.0	25.0	34.3	33.3	9.8	39.8	17.6
10–14		22.5	26.9	3.9	2.8	7.8	25.0	29.4	5.7	48.0
15–19		17.6	15.7	20.6	.9	2.9	6.5	22.5		25.5
20–24		6.9	11.1	17.6		4.9	1.9	18.6		5.9
25–29		2.0	1.9	13.7		2.9	.9	5.9		1.0
30–34			.9	10.8				3.9		
35–39			.9	12.7				2.0		
40–49				10.8				4.9		
50–59				4.9						
60–69				2.0						

* In the cases of three deceased legislators (Gibson, Haudenshield, and Riley), they and their successors have been considered a single legislator. In addition, illness kept several legislators away from Harrisburg for large portions of the session. However, only one Democrat and four Republicans voted on fewer than 500 of the 804 nonunanimous roll calls during the session. Of course, the deviation percentages for each legislator were computed only after subtracting abstentions from total voting opportunities.

Not all the Democratic discipline can be attributed to the two-party struggle in the House, however. The Democrats showed a greater degree of party loyalty than did the Republicans even on those roll calls in which party majorities agreed (Table 30). No party battle rages here, and the constitutional majority necessary for passage is ensured. This particular difference between Democratic and Republican legislators suggests that the great disparity in party-line voting has some explanation other than majority-minority conflict.

To be sure, it is possible that the discipline created on the party votes transferred to nonparty issues. But the deviants on the issues which found the parties in agreement were not the same legislators who left the party majority when the two parties were in opposition. Coefficients of correlation for percentage deviations on these two types of roll call read only .38 for the Democratic legislators and a negative .22 for the Republicans. The mavericks on these issues in which the majority of the parties agree have little about their background or party ties to explain their divergence from party lines. In neither party did deviation on issues of party agreement relate to competitiveness of district, population density or urbanness, or other constituency or personal characteristics. The fifty-three legislators with the lowest deviation percentages do show a median of four years of holding party office, whereas the fifty-three highest scorers show only two years.[15] And the low scorers also have, on the average, an extra session of experience in the House itself. But there the clues run out.

These men who choose the lonely vote against party and the great majority of the chamber may be called the true *idéologues* of the House. They are unwilling to go along, preferring instead the often solitary dictates of conscience or ideological system. They are men and women with intellectual or idiosyncratic bases for personal choice. They may be the inner-directed legislators, the ones guided in decision-making by internalized value systems. One might also argue that they are the legislators who are

15. From this point on, we are dealing only with the 106 legislators of the interview sample.

exceptionally sensitive to stirrings in the constituencies. Were this the case, one would expect to find the incidence of deviation related to constituency characteristics. Such, though, is not the case. Those legislators who left their party ranks on such issues tended, however, to be the same ones who professed to be self-directed trustees when queried about their legislative roles (Table 31). One may at least say that unexplained trustee roles lead

---

TABLE 31

RELATION BETWEEN DEVIATION ON ROLL CALLS IN WHICH PARTIES AGREED AND SELECTION OF LEGISLATIVE ROLE

	Legislators with lowest deviation (N = 53)	Legislators with highest deviation (N = 53)
	Percentage	
I. *Constituency versus judgment*		
Constituency ("delegate")	45.3	32.1
Own judgment ("trustee")	26.4	39.6
Compromise, evasion	28.3	26.4
No information	0	1.9
II. *General role*		
Party-oriented	13.2	3.8
District-oriented	50.9	39.6
Self-oriented	18.9	32.1
None discernible	17.0	22.6
No information	0	1.9

---

to some extent to equally inexplicable trustee voting in the legislature.

On those roll calls in which party majorities *opposed* each other, however, the deviation percentages of the Pennsylvania legislators confirm several earlier studies. The researches of Mac-Rae in the Massachusetts legislature suggest that party regularity is least frequent among those legislators whose margin of electoral victory was the slightest.[16] Because of the close contest they can expect at the next election, they must weigh constituency loyalties (when those loyalties run counter to party wishes) more heavily than the legislator sitting in a sure district. Of the one-half (fifty-three) of the legislators in the sample with the lowest deviation percentages, 45.3 per cent won their seats with less than 60 per cent of the two-party vote. But 67.9 per cent of the highest scorers were under that margin. Taking the gubernatorial race as a reasonable reflection of the long-run party competitiveness of a district, there exists some correlation between the deviation percentage on roll calls with parties opposed and the percentage of two-party vote won by Gov. David Lawrence in the district. The coefficient of correlation for the Republicans is .4847, and for the Democrats it is —.5377. Party competitiveness does tend, apparently, to break down party loyalty and attentiveness.

Related to this hypothesis is another which attempts to explore the cross-fire between constituency and party for the legislator's allegiance. MacRae found party regularity among those Massachusetts legislators whose constituencies were most typical of those their party won. Those elected from districts typical of those the other party usually won and atypical of their own were more likely to cross party lines to woo voters normally predisposed by general socioeconomic characteristics to support candidates of the other party.[17] The fairest test of party typicality in Pennsylvania is probably population density. Chapter 3 established that the Democrats win in the densely settled, urban sectors of the state, whereas the Republicans carry the low-density areas. True to expectations, the Pennsylvania legislators most likely to leave party lines in each party came from the districts atypical of their party's strength (Table 32). The tendency was marked in

16. Duncan MacRae, Jr., "The Relation Between Roll Call Votes and Constituencies in the Massachusetts House of Representatives," *American Political Science Review*, XLVI (1952), No. 4, 1046–1055.
17. *Ibid.* MacRae's standard of typicality was owner-occupancy of dwellings. Republican districts showed the higher percentages, and the Democrats carried the districts of low percentage of owner-occupancy.

both parties, but more clearly in the Democratic. The Democrats from the atypical rural areas were overwhelmingly less responsive to the party call, and Republicans from the closely settled cities shied away from their party majority. Coefficients of correlation here support the data of Table 32. The Democrats show a negative

TABLE 32

RELATION BETWEEN DEVIATION PERCENTAGES ON ROLL
CALLS IN WHICH PARTIES WERE OPPOSED AND THE
URBAN-RURAL NATURE OF THE DISTRICT

	Democrats		Republicans	
Population density	Lowest deviation (N = 27)	Highest deviation (N = 27)	Lowest deviation (N = 26)	Highest deviation (N = 26)
	Percentage			
0–99/sq. mi.	0	18.5	42.3	15.4
100–999	11.1	44.4	38.5	34.6
1,000–9,999	22.2	22.2	11.5	34.6
10,000 and over	63.0	11.1	7.7	15.4
No information	3.7	3.7	0	0

.5500 correlation between population density and deviation percentage; a .4246 coefficient marks the Republicans.[18]

One last indication of the power of constituency over party emerges from the interview data on these 106 legislators of the sample. Whereas 60.4 per cent of the frequent mavericks have lived all their lives in their present county, 77.4 per cent of the least frequent deviants are lifelong residents of the county. The longer the ties have bound, apparently, the tighter they bind.

These are the constituency forces which intrude on the parties' attempts at cohesion; what creates and reinforces that cohesion? Very simply, party creates its own loyalty—a fact seen

18. When the deviation percentage is correlated with the percentage of people in the district living in rural areas, the results are Democrats, .6290; Republicans, −.3668.

with crystal clarity in the Democratic Party (Table 33). Democratic cohesion in the legislature on roll calls in which majorities of the party were in opposition was clearly associated with active

---

TABLE 33

RELATION BETWEEN DEVIATION ON ROLL CALLS IN
WHICH PARTIES WERE OPPOSED AND TYPE OF
PARTY ORGANIZATION AND ACTION IN PRIMARY

	Democrats		Republicans	
	Lowest deviation (N = 27)	Highest deviation (N = 27)	Lowest deviation (N = 26)	Highest deviation (N = 26)
	Percentage			
Party organization				
A and B	100.0	63.0	30.8	57.5
C and D	0	37.0	69.2	42.3
Primary action				
Closed, covert	100.0	77.8	69.2	92.3
Open	0	22.2	30.8	7.7

---

organization and strong party action in the primaries. The twenty-seven Democratic legislators of lowest deviation score had a median of five years of party office, whereas exactly one-half of the twenty-seven high scorers had none at all.

All these associations are reversed in the Republican ranks. Again we have the conflict between party and constituency. Within the Democratic Party, the districts of typicality and sure seats are the very districts of strong party organizations. Not so with the Republicans. Their strongest organizations (in the cities) sit precisely in the areas of party atypicality and electoral failures. Constituency pressures work on the Republican legislator right across party lines and ties, and constituency wins over party. The Republicans from the strong party organizations displayed the least party loyalty in roll calls (Table 33). And, also contrary to the

143

Democrats, the most frequent Republican deviants had the longest records of holding party office—a median of four years, as against none for the twenty-six most loyal legislators. To repeat the most significant conclusion: where constituency influence meets party pressure, it is party, not constituency, which gives way.

Almost as interesting as the factors which make and break party cohesion are those which do not. Personal characteristics—occupation, age, social status, educational level—make no difference. Nor does the number of men elected from the district. Contrary to the suggestions of some writers, experience in the Pennsylvania House has no effect by itself on party cohesion. Freshmen vote as often with the party majority as do the ten-session veterans. And, most impressive of all, the role of the party in recruiting the legislator to run for the legislature and the amount of primary competition he recently faced do not seem to affect his party loyalty. Although general party strength can, in the absence of constituency pressures, produce cohesive party voting, influence in an individual nomination alone is apparently of no avail. The establishment of party responsibility appears to be an infinitely more complicated matter than the mere assertion of party control over the nominating process.

Summary

A state as given to aggressive politics as Pennsylvania is inevitably reflects that party vigor in its legislative politics. Experience within and with strong constituency parties often imparts an intense degree of party loyalty to legislative candidates. When they vote, the legislators display a high degree of party discipline, a discipline heightened by both majority party pressures within the House and by the general strength and values of the constituency parties.

Yet, the parties must share legislative allegiances. Members of the House, their voting records to the contrary, show a surprising reticence in acknowledging their debt to party in appraising their legislative role. The Pennsylvania parties have apparently not yet conquered nonparty, "independent" expectations about legislative behavior. To some extent, the legislator may rationalize his party loyalty in terms of choosing on behalf of his constituency's interests or by reason of his own judgment and then finding *post hoc* that his choice comports well with party goals. Members of a party are brought together by similar constituency pressures or by similar ideological commitments. Party may serve only to rally cohesive constituency interests as far as the individual legislator is concerned.

Since party divisions in the House fall along urban-rural lines, and particularly since cohesion tends to be greatest among big-city Democrats and rural Republicans, what appear to be tightly drawn party lines may instead be the lines of urban-rural conflict. Or they may be the conflicts of the various social and economic groups and interests living in city and country. At the least, the superimposition of metropolitan-nonmetropolitan lines on the party struggle intensifies the struggle and stiffens party lines. When the party axis coincides with the urban-rural axis, one loses sight of which are the party issues and which the urban-rural issues, but the practical effect is to harden the lines of partisan opposition.[19]

The inroads of constituency on party cohesion appear as clearly in Pennsylvania as elsewhere. In those instances of sharpened party differences—the roll calls in which majorities of the two parties oppose each other—legislators leave the party to placate constituency pressures exaggerated by close elections or a threatening socioeconomic electoral base. Where the influence of party and constituency conflict, constituency tends to win out. All the resources of a strong party and all the disciplined control of the recruitment process do not prevail against the constituency's ultimate threat: defeat. Strong local parties and vigorous nominating will not, apparently, serve as a panacea for splintered, nonideological parties.

Still, there remains the impressive over-all degree of party cohesion in the Pennsylvania House. When legislators are not yielding to constituency, they cling to party. Party cohesion pre-

19. Keefe suggests this point in his "Comparative Study of the Role of Political Parties in State Legislatures," *Western Political Quarterly*, IX (1956), No. 3, 736.

vails as the norm. Legislative mores favor it, and considerations of constituency or conscience must overturn it. Party in the legislature is, of course, tolerant and understanding of the problem of the legislator with a "tough district." When he argues that, in reality, the members of the other party elect him, his pleas generally find sympathetic ears in the pragmatists of the party caucus. All other things being equal, however, party expects support on at least the major issues. It does not expect that individual legislators will ride to battle in their separate ways and directions.

What party discipline there is, though, comes not entirely from whip-cracking in the House. The party caucuses do command stern disciplinary measures when necessary, but their threats and pressures probably cannot by themselves create persistent party discipline. It seems probable that that discipline is in part the logical result of a recruitment and election system in which the parties elect men of somewhat similar personal characteristics from similar constituencies with similar interests and political mores. The fact that each party builds most effectively in constituencies with similar characteristics, in other words, minimizes the chances of local loyalties impinging on party cohesion.

Party discipline in the legislature, however, does not equal party responsibility. If the legislative discipline does not expound or support a coherent program known in advance to the voters, responsibility cannot exist. A great gulf yawns in Pennsylvania—and in most other states—between the local, constituency parties and the legislative party. Communication between them is erratic and desultory at best, and, although the legislative party may have to support a state-wide platform or a governor's program, the local parties may freely keep eyes and heart close to local bread-and-butter issues.[20] The unified party with a common ideology—this centralized party of the "responsibility" blueprint—does not exist even in the party system of Pennsylvania.

20. Epstein, *Politics in Wisconsin, op. cit.,* p. 142, suggests that, were local party organizations to intervene more in the votes of the legislator, especially by making elaborate demands on him, they would reduce cohesion in the legislature. Should that be true, the attempt of the constituency party to meet the conditions of party responsibility would destroy its very legislative mechanism.

146

7 • Localism and the Party System

Thus do the Pennsylvania parties perform the classic electing function. In most respects their operations reflect a level of strength and activity matched by the parties of few states. And yet the Pennsylvania parties find their operations hedged about by the limits the constituencies impose. That striking influence which the constituencies enjoy in the party and in the representational system is perhaps the most persistent theme of this study. Constituency expectations shape the nature of the parties, and they dictate the characteristics of the candidates. In the legislature, the constituencies extract a high measure of loyalty from the local sons they send to represent them.

Such localism is, of course, not unknown in the decentralized American party system. But Pennsylvania appears to offer the prototype of a decentralized, localized party system. The effects of that local dominance on the parties are clear. The party organizations in the constituencies are artifacts of their interests and expectations. The kind of organization the party sets up is to a great extent a function of the constituency's two-party division and political culture. The political mores of the urban areas permit and accept aggressive, year-around political organization and intervention in the nominating process. Those of many rural areas do not. More than a few county chairmen in the rural precincts of the state itch to endorse slates of candidates at the primary. Only fear of local reaction prevents them. It is only in their internal organizational matters, such as patterns of leadership, that the parties escape the pressure of the constituency's demands.

Obviously, if the political party is to such an extent the creature of the constituency, it is not the independent political organizer we so freely assume it is. It does not independently set the style of politics or define its own political role and functions. In all its aspects, it must often accede to local interests, to local political mores, and even to local definition of itself. Contrary to the myths of partisans and party leaders, the party as an organization is not entirely or even largely the product of will or sheer hard work in the party ranks. Although, in other words, scholars have been quick to see the effects of a decentralized, localized party system on representation and legislative behavior, they have been slow to recognize its great effects on the parties themselves.

The power of the constituency over the legislative party is no less impressive. Although the parties in Pennsylvania do generate considerable discipline in the state House of Representatives, the chief limit to that discipline comes from the local, constituency pressures. Pennsylvania legislators choose the role of delegate—the mandated agent of the constituency—in greater numbers than do the legislators of comparable states. The defectors on party-line votes come from those districts that most severely threaten their tenure—the districts that have been the most competitive and those which are least typical of the districts the party usually carries. Pennsylvania legislators find it easier to give steadfast party loyalty when they hold safe seats of the socio-economic characteristics to which their party usually appeals. Even rigorous party control of the primary and preprimary selec-

148

tion processes cannot prevail over the pressures of the atypical and marginal constituency.

In addition to their impact on the parties in general, the political demands and necessities of the constituencies have had specific consequences for each of the two parties. The distribution of political cultures between urban and rural areas determines that the elected Democrats will be associated with and enjoy the advantages of well-organized and active party organizations. Constituency insistence on status and success among the legislative candidates, on the other hand, works to the advantage of the Republicans in the recruitment of appealing candidates. This degree of political localism also heightens the inequities present in any system of apportionment or districting. Even the small degree of favoritism shown the rural districts in Pennsylvania takes on greater importance in view of the intense, particularistic local loyalty it magnifies. The usual justifications for representational inequalities—the Burkean and the virtual-representation theories—clearly have little relevance to such a constituency-oriented system.

If this localism of Pennsylvania legislative politics were taking place in a homogeneous political culture, its impact would not be so notable. Sharp differences in the political cultures of Pennsylvania greatly accentuate the localism. Those elusive cultural aspects, related to urbanism and ethnic background, shape differing party types and invest them with differing patterns of activity. They establish the maximum parties of the cities and the minimum parties of the rural parts of the state. They define, that is, differing patterns of political styles in the state. Not only do the parties differ in the configurations of socioeconomic interests they represent, but they differ in the state as a whole in the political image they present in their organization and operation. In the state legislature, Democrats and Republicans represent areas of differing political cultures, as well as of differing interests. What ideological differences there may be between the two legislative parties are reinforced by differences in political style as distinct as the country club and the Tuesday-night bowling league.

149

These variations in political style have their consequences in the legislative process. They may explain something of the nature of urban-rural conflict in the state legislature. In part, that conflict may actually be a clash of political cultures and styles between the men of the city parties and those from the less aggressive and more relaxed rural parties. These differences may be reinforced by differences in the backgrounds of the legislators and in what they seek from politics and public office. From this clash in political styles and from the suspicions they foster, legislators and their observers may see more disagreement on substantive issues than actually exists. At the least, these differences in political style, as they coincide with party lines, may aid the formation of party spirit and discipline in the legislative chamber. ✗

In such a decentralized party system, can the parties achieve any degree of responsibility to a platform or ideology? In view of the considerable party cohesion and discipline the parties generate in the legislature, the question is a fair one. That legislative party loyalty, though, does not support a comprehensive, articulated program. The parties and legislative candidates campaign on issues touching only lightly on ideology or platforms. Party cohesion in the House is largely a reflection of the loyalty to local party—to the party as a party—that one would expect from legislators as thoroughly schooled in local party demands and activity as they. It also shows the reinforcing effects of the party struggle in the legislature. Hence, the greater the number of years in the House, the greater the party cohesion. Furthermore, discipline is greater in the majority party than in the minority.

Yet, from this system, the Pennsylvania parties fashion a reasonable substitute for party responsibility. The state's political system is sufficiently homogeneous to divide the constituencies of the state along social and economic lines. The Democrats capture the large cities and the coal and steel valleys. The Republicans take the districts of rural Pennsylvania. Consequently, each party's legislators represent differing clusters of local interests, personal characteristics and values, and varieties of party and political experience. These differences promote and stiffen party discipline.

150

Legislators from constituencies most typical of their party show the greatest degree of party cohesion in legislative roll-call voting. That fact in itself indicates the constituency basis of party cohesion.

So, the parties achieve an indirect responsibility to an inarticulate ideology—the common interests and goals of the similar constituencies from which they draw their most loyal partisans. It is in the support of this inarticulate ideology and the gubernatorial program, rather than in that of a spelled-out party program, that this party discipline is used. The legislative party merely mobilizes the cohesive party vote from among its basically non-ideological ranks. Unencumbered by any specific electoral commitments of their own, the legislators may respond to the more general urgings of party and constituency on behalf of a program which they did not formulate or support in the election. Party cohesion in the legislature is not the result of prior program commitments, but to a great extent their absence permits the ascendance of party attitudes and loyalties.

In Pennsylvania, then, the discipline the parties generate in the constituencies and the discipline they enforce in the legislature are separate. The model of the responsible party would have the party's disciplinary efforts at the local level directed to the ultimate enactment of a party program into public policy. The model party would direct its local energies to its one, over-riding programmatic mission. Not so the Pennsylvania parties. The discipline and cohesion of the legislative votes are curiously disembodied from the politics of the constituencies. This discipline is principally created and enforced by residual party loyalties, by the persistence of the party caucus, and by a patronage-powerful governor.

So, local party discipline exists largely for the purely local purposes of these self-sufficient constituency parties. It is true that some constituency parties use their power over the primary and local elections to purge the legislator who flouts party discipline in Harrisburg. Most, however, use it to maintain control of the office as a part of its elective patronage or to ensure the legislator's receptivity to party suggestions. The loyalty it demands is loyalty

151

to the local party—loyalty in the form of activity in the party, possibly contributions to it, attention to its local interests and those of the constituency, and fealty to its leadership. The local party in such a politics of localism, and particularly in a state so given to a politics of immediate reward, seeks more ardently than usual the perquisites of power as ends in themselves.

Under the influence of the constituency, the local party in reality merges its interests and personality with those of the constituency. For example, candidates, in discussing their concept of the legislative role, often fail to see any conflict between party and constituency. As they represent so accurately local interests and expectations, they also represent the party. Party power at the local level is at the service of the constituency. Control of the primary permits the party to cater to the locality by picking candidates who mirror local characteristics and by balancing tickets in deference to local and provincial loyalties. By merging its political life with the constituency this fully, the party reinforces that localism. As the party so uses its local power and ability to control the nomination process, it works against the development of a state-wide party power or ideology. Locally directed party power, even over the primary, may thus work against the development of party responsibility in the state legislature.

Clearly, these local party organizations fail to meet the usual standards of the ideological, policy-oriented, responsible political party. They must be evaluated in more modest terms. We conventionally associate party strength with the ability to win elections. If by "strength" we mean disciplined, well-manned party organizations, able to control their nominations, then this study indicates that strength is associated not with victory but with political culture. Victory does not produce this sort of organization, nor will such an organization inevitably produce victory. It appears among both winning and losing parties in urban, densely populated districts. The ability of a party to win elections is in itself, of course, a relevant fact about it in such a pragmatic party system as ours. We cannot, however, assume that certain desired organizational and functional traits will accompany the winning parties.

152

The justest criterion by which one can appraise the political parties in such a state as Pennsylvania, then, is probably their ability to control the political activities surrounding the selection of public officials. Even though they must operate within the expectations of the local political culture, the most effective of them will exclude nonparty groups from a share of the function. They are, furthermore, able to exclude nonparty elites from control of the party organization. Their leaders will be the formal, open, official leadership of the party. They will make few concessions to the demands for intraparty democracy. In their control of the selection of public officials, they will yield to no competing party faction or nonparty group the power, or even a share of the power, to govern the prospects of would-be candidates.

Finally, the role of the Pennsylvania parties in the broader representational system deserves brief comment. The parties dominate the processes of informal organization that go on within the formal system of legislative representation. That representative role they perform in two separate ways. The second of them, the organization of majorities within the legislature itself, we have discussed. Before that, however, the parties have dominated the recruitment of candidates across the state. Not even the direct primary has seriously challenged that domination or forced the party to share it with its registrants. In effect, the parties control the primary through control of the selection processes which go on before it. Rarely must they fight powerful opponents in the primary, and even more rarely do they lose a fight. The Pennsylvania parties are undeniably the local talent scouts for democracy. And, given the absence of party competitiveness in so many areas of the state, it is no exaggeration to say that in reality the parties choose a vast majority of the Pennsylvania legislators.

In making these choices, the parties select in the name of the constituency and of its demands. They recruit and endorse candidates so much "of" the constituency that their loyalty to its interests needs little prompting or supervision. That is just as well, since the attention of the party and the local voters shifts quickly from the legislator once the election is won. By selecting men of the social characteristics of the district, in other words,

153

Appendix A

Note on Method

Whatever progress political science has made in the postwar years toward developing explanatory theories and generalizations about politics has been in large part the result of a concern for more rigorous and refined procedures. This emphasis on more precise concepts, more careful and explicit method, and more cautious interpretation of data has occasioned some dissent within the fraternity, largely on the grounds that it reflects a misguided attempt to lead political science to an illusory "scientism." If, however, the goal of scholarship is knowledge, then the knowledge it produces must be precisely and clearly stated, must have relevance in similar contexts, must be capable of repeated discovery and expansion, and must be free from willful and illogical interpretation of data.

Although the methods and techniques employed in this study are neither new nor esoteric, I set them down for two purposes. Adequately warned, the reader may take my methods into account in evaluating the worth of what they have produced. Second, the scholar who wishes to use and improve on them to repeat or build on any part of this study has a point of departure.

Procedures

Above all, the procedures of this study reflect my conviction of the necessity for field work in research in political science. Field work poses any manner of difficulties for the scholar— elusive interviewees, the demands of time and money, data that do not fit neatly into categories, and even (and not the least of it) the scarcely digestible food of small-town America. But a great body of data that never finds its way into census reports, vote totals, or legislative journals awaits the political scientist who goes out to seek it. His alternative is to permit the availability and accessibility of other data to determine his scholarly priorities. In the study of politics and political parties, we are in danger of overworking limited bodies of data with elaborate methods. The need for the expansion of our data by field observation seems to me to be clear.

Before a fuller explanation of the field work, a word about the other data-gathering procedures may be in order. A large share of the material on the constituencies themselves was pieced together from census data. Fortunately, all of the Pittsburgh and most of the Philadelphia ward lines (from which legislative districts are constructed) coincide with census tract lines. Census data can also be rearranged to conform to constituency boundaries where the constituencies comprise a county, a city, or a county minus a city. But, where districts are a part of a county or a part of a city not divided into census tracts, no human ingenuity can translate the census data into constituency data.

Primary and general election data for the legislative constituencies are readily available, either in the *Pennsylvania Manual* or from the excellent Bureau of Elections of the Pennsylvania Department of State. Much of the data on party registration by legislative district, however, had to be ferreted out of county courthouses. The data on roll-call votes in the 1958 session of the House of Representatives come from the House *Journals*.

156

The sample of 106 legislators was interviewed in Harrisburg in the early months of the 1959 session, well before the legislative calendars became crowded. No appointments for the interviews were arranged, on the theory that requests for appointments invite refusals, procrastination, and rehearsed answers. Since Pennsylvania legislators have no offices, interviews had to be conducted in the halls, cloakrooms, and at the desks of the legislators before and after sessions. We planned the interviews to last no longer than one-half hour; the tersest few divulged the information we sought in fifteen or twenty minutes, but others expanded their remarks for an hour or more. The average interview lasted a shade under one-half hour. In this interview, we obtained the data on the legislator's social characteristics, political career and history, recruitment to run for the legislature, activities in the legislature, and his understanding of the role of the legislator. One legislator who was absent from the session because of illness was interviewed at his home later in the summer.

The major burden, however, involved the interviewing in the seventy-eight constituencies of the sample. These districts are scattered over forty-seven of the state's sixty-seven counties. In each constituency, work began with the interviewing of the candidate defeated in November, 1958. These interviews paralleled in time and scope those with the legislators in Harrisburg; in fact, identically worded questions were usually used. Then, to get general background, a "feel" for the local politics, and specific data on the constituency and the parties (party policy on intervention in the primary, for instance), we talked to knowledgeable local informants. The question of whom to seek out was one we played by ear in each district. We usually interviewed the two party chairmen and local newspapermen, but a composite list of interviewees would include local officeholders, courthouse habitués, other defeated candidates, local lawyers, embittered or disenchanted politicians, party officials, teachers and professors, trade-association and interest-group officials, labor leaders, and clergymen. Frequently, too, the morgues of local newspapers provided invaluable background.

This sort of personal interviewing poses formidable problems. As a method of securing data, it has nothing of the comforting, if misleading, concreteness and accuracy of reliance on electoral data. It necessitates dealing with people often personally involved in the information one is seeking. The possibilities for inaccuracy are limitless—the misunderstood question or reply, the willful falsehood, the calculated or innocent half-truth, or the simple ignorance of the respondent. However, I strongly suspect that those whose fears are entirely second-hand grossly overestimate the pitfalls that threaten the interviewer. Intentional deceit is not a serious problem, and the researcher does have a number of ways to cross-check information. Especially if one avoids the area of intention and motivation and confines himself to ascertaining concrete data, his problems are within control. Skillful questioning can at least clarify questions and answers, but election totals—those unimpeachable figures to which we so freely defer—may contain all manner of definitions of what the voters intended their votes to represent.

The average political scientist probably seriously overestimates the secretiveness of the average politician. I found them surprisingly and engagingly cooperative. Every legislator we approached consented to be interviewed, and all but five of the defeated candidates we reached were agreeable.[1] Few local informants whom we approached refused to answer our questions. The usual reaction was one of pleasure and flattery at being sought out; some of the representatives in Harrisburg who were not in the interview sample actually expressed disappointment at being omitted. The candor of our informants was, furthermore, often breathtaking, even though none of the interviews was off the record.[2] Politics become as routine to those who live them as the facts of everyday life, and they discuss them as openly and

    1. A total of 105 were interviewed in the sample; the one omitted, a recent heart-attack victim, could not be reached. A total of ninety-five of the 104 defeated candidates were interviewed (two legislators were unopposed). A detailed accounting of the absentees can be found in Chapter 4.
    2. We did, however, promise them anonymity; their observations and answers have never been attributed to them.

matter-of-factly as others might discuss a charitable fund-raising drive or the local Little League standings.[3]

The interviewer is, however, not completely at the mercy of any one of his informants. In this study, we interviewed a legislator, a defeated candidate, two party chairmen, and assorted community leaders and knowledgeable citizens in most of the districts of the sample. Aside from the cross-checks provided by a number of sources, the criteria of internal consistency and general plausibility helped to check the information from any one source. As for the accuracy and fairness of the information our interviewing yielded, I can say that I am aware of only one of the 105 legislators deliberately misleading us, and this deception was, I believe, limited to the facts of his political history and his decision to run for the House.

The interviewing of this study, it should be clear, did not at any point involve sampling community opinion or attitudes. Its purpose was solely to elicit such information as that on the party recruitment of candidates, the nature of factionalism in a party, the religion of the defeated candidates, the legislator's influence in his party, the predominant ethnic groups in the district, and the like. At only one point did we try to ascertain attitudes; both legislators and defeated candidates were asked three open-ended questions on their perception of the legislator's role and his relation to his party.

---

3. Occasionally we were rebuffed by local politicos. The reader may be interested in the following scene recorded by one of the interviewers on the project:

Scene: Interviewer approaches Pittsburgh ward chairman, introduces himself, and explains for whom he is working (the author) and something of the nature of the project.

Ward Chairman: "If this Hunky wants information from me, he'll have to pay for it. I got a hell of a lot more degrees than him. I'll write a book myself. That's a stupid thing—to go around askin' people for information."

Interviewer exits silently.

The Sample

Because neither the time nor the money was available for interviewing all 210 legislators and all 210 defeated candidates and seeking data in all the 154 legislative constituencies, I resorted to a 50 per-cent sample for this interviewing. The sample taken for the study represents the constituencies, rather than the legislators, so as not to split the representatives elected from the multimember districts. Once a constituency was chosen for the sample, all its legislators and all its defeated candidates were automatically included. The 50 per-cent figure for the sample represents an arbitrary compromise between complete coverage and the limitations of time, money, and the human spirit.

The sample typifies all 154 constituencies in the following ways: by party of legislator, by number of legislators chosen by the district, and by a combined urban-rural and area measure.[4] Tables 34 and 35 indicate the distributions in sample and universe of these factors. They disclose a sampling close to the 50 per-cent standard in all categories, and Table 35 shows furthermore that no violence is done the sample by cross-tabulating within the factors that determined the sample. Of course, where numbers of constituencies in any single cell drop as low as some of these do, distortions inevitably result.[5]

To check the validity of the sample, it was compared after the completion of data-collecting with all 154 constituencies to determine its representativeness in dimensions that were not considered in the initial selection of the sample. The sample, for

4. This three-part category does not employ the census definition of "urban" and "rural." Rather, it expresses an attempt to combine concepts of "urbanness" and area distribution into few enough categories to be useful in the sampling. The three categories used were: (1) *rural districts*—those which are by themselves undivided counties (the small, less populous, and predominantly rural counties); (2) *mixed urban-rural districts*—those in counties with more than one legislative district (the more populous and urban counties); (3) *metropolitan districts*—those in Allegheny and Philadelphia counties.

5. The problems of drawing an accurate sample from the small number of three- and four-member districts are virtually insoluble. However, an attempt was made to achieve an accurate sample of combined three- and four-man districts.

160

instance, includes 51 per cent of the constituencies with populations of less than 45,000 per legislator, 51 per cent of those between 45,000 and 54,999, and 50 per cent of those with 55,000 or more.

TABLE 34

COMPARISON OF 50 PER-CENT SAMPLE WITH
UNIVERSE OF DISTRICTS

	Universe	Sample	
		Number	Percentage
I. *Total districts*	154	78	51
One-member	113	57	50
Two-member	31	16	52
Three-member	5	3	60
Four-member	5	2	40
II. *Total legislators*	210	106	50
Democrats	108	54	50
Republicans	102	52	51
III. *Districts from rural counties* *	40	20	50
One-member	34	17	50
Two-member	6	3	50
IV. *Districts from mixed urban-rural counties* *	66	34	52
One-member	43	22	51
Two-member	17	9	53
Three-member	4	2	50
Four-member	2	1	50
V. *Districts from Allegheny and Philadelphia counties* *	48	24	50
One-member	36	18	50
Two-member	8	4	50
Three-member	1	1	100
Four-member	3	1	33

* Category defined in Footnote 4.

TABLE 35

LEGISLATORS, BY DISTRICT AND PARTY, IN SAMPLE AND UNIVERSE

Legislators	Universe	Sample	
		Number	Percentage
I. *Elected from one-member districts*	113	57	50
Democrats	65	33	51
Republicans	48	24	50
II. *Elected from two-member districts*	62	32	52
Democrats	28	15	54
Republicans	34	17	50
III. *Elected from three-member districts*	15	9	60
Democrats	12	6	50
Republicans	3	3	100
IV. *Elected from four-member districts*	20	8	40
Democrats	3	0	0
Republicans	17	8	47

Appendix B

Categories and Indexes

The most exasperating aspect of this study was the necessity of formulating the categories and measurements necessary for its execution. Wherever possible, I have used measurements and criteria used by earlier scholars; these have been noted in the text and need no further elaboration here. But, especially in the study of local party organizations and operations, few earlier guides existed.

Any impeccably systematic study of local political parties will have to await the accumulation of resources far greater than this project enjoyed. The problems of judging 156 local political parties and their functions with limited personnel and time are as sobering as they are perplexing. A trained researcher could over a long period make the first-hand observations and hold the lengthy, systematic interviews which we were unable to do. Some of the assessments of local party reported here rest on personal observation, but they are in general based on information supplied by local informants. They are, therefore, doubly impressionistic; they are based on my impressions of the impressions of interviewees.

The purpose of these remarks is not to apologize for the data so obtained and reported, but rather to alert the reader to their limitations. It seems to me that, instead of waiting for the best possible of all scholarly worlds, the scholar must set out to do the best job he can with the resources available. More precise and elegant methods may be used when time and funds permit. Every scholarly method has its limitations and difficulties. Methodological wisdom lies, not in a futile search for perfection, but in the recognition of any method's shortcomings and the limits they impose on interpretation.

In view of these problems, I have tried to minimize the resultant difficulties by two simple precautions. First of all, the categories adopted are simple and uncomplicated. In most sets, only two or three categories have been established; distinctions are broad and general to provide an especially charitable margin of error. Second, I have whenever possible used as categories the natural types of the Pennsylvania party system. The distinctions and differences represented are not, in other words, arbitrary or a priori; they grow out of real distinctions perceptible in Pennsylvania politics.

The Riddle of Party: Chapter 3

No conceptual problem caused more anguish than the definition of types of party organization. I began with five types, but, since the last and lowest order of organization applied to so few cases, it was combined with the fourth. These categories represent an assessment of the nature of the party organization itself. "Organization" had to be defined quite apart from the question of whether the party's candidates win public office and apart from the nature of party activity in the primary and preprimary selection. The five party organizational types, representing degrees of development in the party's organizational apparatus, reflect two main criteria: the staffing of the organization and its internal control and discipline.

164

"Staffing" refers to the extent to which positions in the party hierarchy are manned by active officers and committeemen. It also takes into account the continuity of the activity: do the partisans work through the year or are they spurred to action only by an election? "Internal control and discipline" refers to the distribution of power within party organizations—whether control of the organization is centralized in the party chairman or executive committee or whether, at the other extreme, it is dispersed into the hands of local leaders or influential committeemen. Such a continuum of power distribution within the organization rules out the possibility of intraparty democracy, but, for better or worse, it can in Pennsylvania be ruled out safely.

The original five categories and their descriptions are:

A   These are the party organizations in which all committee positions are occupied by alert and active committeemen who maintain regular party activity, even at non-election times. Frequently, party clubs or headquarters rooms testify to the continuous operations. The organization is also under the centralized control of the party leadership, and committeemen and all subordinates must carry out their decisions and support their chosen candidates. Those who do not may lose party rewards and favor.

B   In these organizations, most (generally two-thirds or more) of the committeemen maintain an active role at the grass roots, although their activity at other than election time is sporadic and unreliable. Central control and discipline may be halfhearted and fleeting. The recalcitrant committeeman may not even be purged or in any way disciplined for defying the party leadership.

C   These organizations are getting along with half or less of the committeemen active in contacting residents, campaigning, or simply "talking up" local party affairs. What activity the organization engages in happens almost entirely at elections; between elections, few signs

165

of life are visible. In these organizations, the central leadership of, say, a county chairman is asserted, but committeemen are fairly free to accept or reject it. Few sanctions will befall them if they reject it, especially since no real system of patronage or officeholding rewards attach to party activity.

D Very little committee activity marks these organizations. In fact, probably less than one-third of the committeemen show any activity. Some of their positions may be vacant or go to the recipients of a few unsolicited write-in votes. What activity there is is found entirely at elections. Centralized control within the organization is virtually nonexistent. Party leadership has few or no sanctions available, and contact between leadership and many committeemen has probably broken down.

E What organization exists at this level exists on paper. The party organization is demoralized, with virtually no committee activity and many committee vacancies. What little organizational activity there is comes from the chairman and perhaps a handful of men who run the organization. Since there is in reality no organization, the issue of control and discipline is moot.

The last category is combined with the one preceding it in the tables of the text. Where party organizations displayed characteristics of two categories, they were placed in the category they fitted better.

Measurement of party activity in the primary and preprimary selection process posed less serious problems. The party's role in the primary could be determined on the single issue of the degree of support it gave a chosen candidate or slate of candidates. Popular usage in Pennsylvania politics also provided a general system of categories. They are described in the text of Chapter 3. For the party's preprimary recruitment role it was necessary to draw up the following categories:

166

Systematic This pattern of recruiting involves formally sifting through candidate possibilities, even interviewing them or their sponsors, and organizing an approved ticket, usually in advance of the first date for filing petitions.

Moderate Recruitment of this variety implies a less formal and systematic process in which party leaders sometimes recruit candidates and sometimes passively accept or reject already-declared candidates. More often than not, this recruitment means putting a partisan seal of approval on self-starting candidates.

Sporadic Recruitment here is that type of party action usually limited to attempts to fill the ticket if no self-selected candidate emerges. The party rarely, if ever, does anything more than this or make an occasional attempt to discourage patently undesirable candidates.

Legislative Roles and Issues: Chapter 6

To a considerable extent, the "moderate" category embraces that vast, intermediate range of recruiting that falls between the extremes of the first and third types.

Some explanation of the role categories used in Table 28 is in order. In Group I, the category, "compromise, evasion," includes these responses: evasion, confusion, refusal or inability to see the dilemma, an insistence on compromising two alternatives, and a subordination of both to party wishes. In Group II, "hostile, weak" responses include assertions of independence, opposition to party and party discipline, rejection of obligation to party, and only nominal loyalty. "Moderate" responses indicate loyalty on some issues, on platform issues, on special party issues only, or loyalty dependent on party help in the district. The "strong" responses were those in which fealty to the party was unqualified. Group III represents an attempt to classify respondents' *primary* responsibility as a legislator, based on their responses to all three questions. The fact that it is my reinterpretation of the data ex-

167

plains the discrepancy between these data and those in Group I. The "none-discernible" category includes those who were confused, vague, or evasive and those who ranked all three options equally.

Finally, some explanation of the division in Chapter 6 of campaign issues into "local" and "nonlocal" would not be amiss. "Local" issues include the following: general fair treatment or assistance for the district; issues of home rule or local government for the district; public improvements for it (dams, parks, roads, bridges, water, flood control, etc.); opposition to local proposals (fluoridation, public housing, expressways, wage tax, etc.); tax relief for the locality; concern about the growth of special governmental authorities or "districts" in the locality; industrial development and general economic rehabilitation; and defense of the district against the demands of other localities (usually Pittsburgh or Philadelphia). The "nonlocal" issues embraced all other types: general issues, good-government issues, partisan issues, issues of personal qualification, ideological issues, and general policy issues.

Index

D

175

Index

178